PRAISE FOR *LOWLY*

"Identity. Belonging. Significance. *Lowly* gives us a deep glance into the world of adolescence and bullying with grit and grace. With the eyes of a parent and the expertise of a youth worker, Laura Angaroni masterfully takes us into the dark places of the teen heart and leads us to a place of redemption and grace. *Lowly* is a hopeful read for teens and parents affected by the world of bullying."

— JJ JONES,
FAMILY DISCIPLESHIP PASTOR,
FELLOWSHIP NASHVILLE,
FRANKLIN CAMPUS

"We really love *Lowly*. Laura expressed the feelings of a young girl so remarkably, along with some wonderful humor and a beautiful life lesson on forgiveness. We give *Lowly* a BIG thumbs-up and look forward to seeing all the Lord has in store for Laura as a writer."

— RUSS AND LINDA MURPHY,
RUSS MURPHY MINISTRIES;
RUSS IS AN AWARD-WINNING INSPIRATIONAL
SINGER-SONGWRITER AND AUTHOR OF *NOT ALONE:
FINDING THE LOVE OF YOUR LIFE*

LOWLY

LAURA P. ANGARONI

Lowly
Copyright © 2016 Laura P. Angaroni

Published by
Deep River Books
Sisters, Oregon
www.deepriverbooks.com

All rights reserved. This book or any portion thereof may not be reproduced or used in any manner whatsoever without the express written permission of the publisher except for the use of brief quotations in a book review.

This is a work of fiction. Names, characters, businesses, places, events, and incidents are either the products of the author's imagination or used in a fictitious manner. Any resemblance to actual persons, living or dead, or actual events is purely coincidental.

ISBN: 9781632694256
Library of Congress: 2016959057
Cover design by Connie Gabbert
Printed in the USA

For Craig
You are my safe place.

For my Oak Cliff friends
You provide laughter and prayer when I need it most.
I left the S at the end of Bisons just for you.

Dear Kimberly,
I'm so glad you're in my life, Sunshine.
Happy reading!
Laura

TABLE OF CONTENTS

Chapter 1 9
Chapter 2 21
Chapter 3 33
Chapter 4 41
Chapter 5 51
Chapter 6 65
Chapter 7 75
Chapter 8 83
Chapter 9 89
Chapter 10 95
Chapter 11 105
Chapter 12 113
Chapter 13 125
Chapter 14 133
Chapter 15 147

Chapter 16..161
Chapter 17..169
Chapter 18..183
Chapter 19..195
Chapter 20..205
Chapter 21..217
Chapter 22..227
Chapter 23..233
Chapter 24..249
Epilogue..263
Acknowledgments...................................271
Author's Page.....................................275

CHAPTER 1

> *Meanwhile, this is the season when most of the people who live in Oak Cliff aren't worrying too much about things. Autumn touches the woods of Kessler . . . especially gently. It'll be enough to get in the car and just ride with the falling leaves and the first chill of the winter and the sharp, sweet scent of the season.*
> *Around dusk is a good time.*
>
> — Warren Leslie, *The Dallas Morning News*, October 1949

"Lola! Nice, Christian girls don't use those words. The only people who use them aren't smart enough to come up with alternatives." Mom puts plenty of emphasis on the word *Christian* as she enters the kitchen.

"Fine! But I'm bleeding. Would it be okay if, just this once, I contemplate my stupidity later?" My sarcasm overflows in response to her correction, imitating the blood from my cut. Even so, I feel a twinge of shame at my verbal slip. I try to hide this from her, of course, though I know she's right.

Still, she needs to give me a break. Doesn't she realize I've cut my finger chopping carrots for *her*? It's got to be worth at least two stitches. It's unbelievable that she's lecturing me about profanity while I'm bleeding all over the place.

Drip, drip, drip. My blood decorates the floor in macabre polka dots. If it wasn't so excruciating, I might become distracted by the odd symmetry of the design.

"I don't care if you've lost a finger. Don't use that tone with me!" She rounds the breakfast bar and does a double take at the carnage. "Oh, no. Let me get you something to apply pressure—it looks like you might need stitches! I'm taking you to the hospital." She rushes off to find her car keys, forgetting to get me a paper towel. I reach to tear one off the roll with one hand while I think on the futility of her remark about my language. That cat was let out of the bag long ago.

Let's take the swear word, for instance. If she only knew what I endure hearing and seeing at school every single day, she'd have a heart attack. If she and Dad didn't want me to pick up bad words, they should've enrolled me in a private, parochial school in a place where I didn't speak the language—from day one of kindergarten. Along the same lines, a classmate educated me on the facts of life by using impolite slang while at recess in the first grade.

I didn't believe the little twerp, but it happened nonetheless.

My mom is naïve.

But on second thought, she did say I could use alternatives. I know plenty of Spanish curse words and even a few French. Would that work?

The thought makes me want to roll my eyes at myself.

Maybe I just need to get a little more creative.

My name is Lola.

I'm not a showgirl, obviously. (Dear Barry Manilow, I'll never forgive you for writing "Copacabana.")

I'm not sure what my parents were thinking when they gave me such an outdated name, but they say they wanted to honor a favorite aunt who died a few years before I was born. This is no great consolation for me and no great tribute for the aunt. After all, I'm me—imperfect in the full sense of the word.

My family and I live in a part of Dallas called Oak Cliff, a substantial portion on the southwestern side of the city. Even though Cliffites take a perverse pride in being from the area, it's considered the wrong side of the tracks. But the truth is, we're just living our lives in a semishabby, semisafe, and semihappy environment like so many other city dwellers.

I've lived here my entire life (all sixteen and a half years). These streets are mine as only a place overly familiar can be. I empathize with them because their gray, potholed, poorly patched state make a fitting picture of my psyche at the end of the last school year.

At this moment, the streets are rolling under the tires of my mom's beige Ford Fairmont as she drives me to school for the start of the 1981–82 year. In the low light of early morning, I watch as deep green St. Augustine lawns, the few flowers that can survive a Texas summer, and tidy little brick and clapboard houses scroll by. As we approach Sunset High School, home of the Bisons, the houses become a little less tidy and a little more unkempt.

My sliced-up finger throbs.

I'm not a super chatty girl, especially in the morning, but I must be even quieter than usual, because Mom asks how I'm feeling.

"What do you think, Lola? Are you ready?" Her tone is soft and appropriate for this early time of day.

I'm not sure how to reply, because, well, I'm not exactly excited. I am purposeful. Things haven't always gone well—mainly due to ongoing harassment from a couple of boys in my classes—but I want to have a positive attitude about heading back. And I have a glimmer of an idea to make things better. I've got to get rid of the Demented Duo or die trying. The school just isn't big enough for the three of us. Meanwhile, I'll try to tamp down on my anger at their treatment despite how much it humiliates me.

Who are the Demented Duo, you're wondering. Matthew Morrison and Luke Owens, labeled as such back in middle school, say things too disgusting to repeat to my mother, or anyone else for that matter. So although Mom would like to know more about my feelings about school, I would rather not start discussing my history with them, including public putdowns about my physical characteristics, my Christianity, and my virginity, a conversation that's sure to embarrass us both. Anyway, Mom doesn't know they treat me like scum, and she doesn't know I don't handle it well. I mean, nice girls don't curse, right? Once Matthew made me so mad that I shot the finger at him.

I harbor a lot of guilt over this.

And my mom's right. A nice, Christian girl doesn't say those words (or make those gestures). Like the song says, I need to let my light shine. In other words, I need to let my faith shine through, but that doesn't happen when people are terrified of your temper or offended by your words. My faith is real, but only those closest to me know this. I can't blame others for judging by my reactions alone.

Has that happened? Have I been judged? I'm not positive that it has, but it's a logical guess. I'm far from the most popular girl in school. If I lack popularity because I'm a Christian, that's fine. If I lack popularity because people are afraid of me, that's not.

I lean back in the car and sigh as I look out the window. "Can you pray for me today, Mom?" Frankly, that's all I can share.

She agrees and tells me she loves me. I reciprocate the love. She's a good mom even though she sometimes asks too many questions.

How *do* I feel about going back to school?

I *am* happy about seeing some friends whom I've missed over the summer, in particular Charlotte. We don't attend the same church, so between family vacations, mission trips, and a boring part-time job dusting glass shelves at a gift shop for the geriatric crowd, I haven't gotten to spend as much time with her as I would like.

We roll to a stop at the drop-off point, and a further damper is placed on my mood in the form of a cancerous growth: a humongous white addition that's supposed to be the new main entrance of our high school. I'm forced to behold it in all its glory because I'm arriving early for drill team. Dad says that some snooty architect hired by some snooty school board subcommittee member thought our beautiful circa 1925 building needed modernization.

"It's ugly. I think I'll call it the Malignant Tumor," I observe.

"It's not so bad, Lola."

My eyes widen at Mom's lack of indignation over the visual monstrosity, but she can't see my look of incredulity. Probably for the best.

"Bye, Mom!" I shout as I slide out of the car. She waves at me over her shoulder as she begins to pull away. I turn to go, but before I can blink, I find myself on the ground.

"Aargh," I growl under my breath.

I roll my body to sit on the concrete and survey the damage. Now, on top of the cut to my finger, I've skinned my palms. I'm not sure what I tripped over (maybe my own feet), but it stings. I wince and my eyes water a bit, but I have a feeling they're watering more from the embarrassment of falling in front of the few other drill team members sleepily staggering toward the door than the slight addition to the pain.

I hear a snicker as one of the senior girls passes me and look up to see Joy Sanchez, the drill team captain's best friend, with a smirk directed at me.

"Way to go," she says. She's had a chip on her shoulder ever since she didn't make officer last spring.

I give an impertinent nod and a fake smile to her back as she saunters off; then I pull myself up and dust the grit off my palms onto my shorts. I'm pretty positive my face is now brighter than the fast-rising sun, reflecting my mood.

Before I can mouth off after Joy's retreating form and make the situation worse, however, Annie arrives, distracting me by trotting up in drill-team-standard practice leotard and bright purple shorts that match mine. Her chestnut hair, bound up in curlers, and a bandana bounce as she moves. I'm glad for her arrival and her help; I need her sympathy and the redirection of my thoughts from a fast-blooming fantasy of punching Joy in her smart mouth. To top it off, my tumble caused the contents of my backpack to make a run for it as if they've a life of their own. But Annie and I are in hot pursuit; they don't stand a chance. We capture, subdue, and force the fugitive supplies back in my now one-handled bag.

"Ignore her, Lola. You know what a witch she can be. Are you okay?"

"Witch? She's a shriveled, dust-covered, one-hundred-year-old soul in a semiattractive seventeen-year-old body. I don't like Joy, but I'll try. Her name has not been prophetic, has it?" I take a few breaths while I try to switch gears, "Anyway, thanks for the help. How was your summer?" My voice still sounds a little strained even as I internally congratulate myself on my ability to pinpoint Joy's essence without using the b-word—I'm sure my mom would be proud.

"Huh. Um, just great." Annie's normal, infectious exuberance seems to have wilted in the last few seconds.

We continue to fill each other in on our respective summers; then I notice her fingers playing with the strap on her purse like a harpist without rhythm. Her large green eyes dart east, west, and every other point on the compass.

"Is anything wrong?" I ask.

"No, nothing! Although . . . I just remembered . . . I forgot something in my car, and . . . and I need to go get it or I'll be late." She passes me the last of my errant belongings (a few dusty pencils); then her words fade as she turns and stumbles off toward the parking lot.

I stare after her in confusion, gather my thoughts, and resume my walk to the gym with a little more awareness of potential trauma in my path.

"Lola! Wait!" suddenly floats from the air in a bright voice I would know anywhere.

I turn around to behold one of my favorite people in the world jogging toward me, silky blonde ponytail trailing in the wind. Charlotte! She runs up and gives me a hug, making me stagger and laugh in surprise. She lets go with a chuckle.

My mood suddenly takes an upturn.

I'm positive I wouldn't make it through high school without Charlotte. We've been friends since junior high, where I discovered she's one of the most honest—but kindest—people you'll ever meet. She's the only person I know who can just spout out the truth and not offend. I think that's an unusual gift.

"Hey there! I've been missin' you and your big Lola words," she jokes as she walks with me.

"I missed you too, but I can't seem to help using them every now and then. Should I apologize?" I shrug in a manner I hope is self-effacing. Come to think of it, "self-effacing" is probably a big Lola word.

"Pfft. It wouldn't be such a problem if you hadn't taught them to Earley at some point. I'm just kiddin' around with you anyway. You know that, right?"

"I know." My gaze flits past her to the parking lot where Annie is parked. "Charlotte, sorry to change the subject, but I just saw Annie, and she was acting a little stray-ange. Do you know what's going on?"

"Oh, yeah." Charlotte vigorously nods, raises one sandy eyebrow, and leans in to continue in a quieter voice, "She went with a group of people to the drive-in on Jefferson over the weekend.

Shelly and her boyfriend were there. I imagine Annie's hoping to be as late as possible in order to spend as little time as possible around Shelly. I don't even want to think about how angry Shelly's sure to be today. She's bad enough on a good day."

"What *happened?*" I whisper back, cringing at the thought of an angry Shelly, our drill team captain. Rob is Shelly's long-time boyfriend, and she's possessive of him to say the least. Actually, I'm pretty tired of Shelly and her attitude, but I guess she's a good captain from a technical standpoint. Moreover, I'm thinking it's not a bad thing in the present case, her stream is overflowing with self-confidence to the point of obnoxiousness. Despite this, her run-in with Annie will likely put our supreme Bisonette on the warpath.

"We don't have time. I'll have to tell you later." Charlotte gives me a mild, quelling look and a small shake of the head.

I guess I have no choice but to let it go for now. So I give her the one-armed girlfriend hug for comfort, and we continue on our way. I'm so glad to see Charlotte that even the thought of our captain turning into Medusa isn't enough to bring me down.

We enter the girls' gym to the sight and sound of willowy, five-foot-eleven-inch Shelly dancing around by herself. Believe it or not, she's singing a self-composed song of her many virtues. I told you she's overflowing with confidence. Did I just hear the words "heavenly thighs"?

She needs to work on her lyrics, but you've got to hand it to the girl—she's creative. Anyway, she seems happy, so drill team may go better than expected.

Nope. I quickly find my meager hope was just that.

It happens when Annie tries to sneak into an empty space next to me in line. All at once, Shelly stops the announcements and with supernatural grace leaps off the platform; her black, waist-length hair billows out in a halo. Megaphone in hand, she marches toward us as if it's halftime on the football field.

"Two demerits, Annie!" She thunders through it directly into Annie's face. I'm pretty sure she's startled some geese in Canada. I am certainly startled. Her bellowing catches me by surprise, and I jump about a foot. Annie's face starts to crumple, and my blood boils.

"What's wrong with you!" My mouth seems to have a mind of its own.

Shelly responds by carefully, daintily placing the megaphone on the floor and pivoting in my direction in order to send me her patented death-by-snakes glare. I'm surprised I'm not reduced to a sizzling black dot on the gym floor at once.

"One demerit for you, Lola."

"What's that? I can't hear you." I insert a bit of irony into my voice before continuing, "Why am I getting a demerit anyway? You're the one shouting into people's faces."

"Another demerit for you, Lola. You shouldn't be disrespectful, and you need to stay out of this. It's not your business." She exudes sanctimoniousness. And she's right about it not being my business, but she's cruel as well. I wish Mrs. Stevens were here to overrule her, but our faculty sponsor is nowhere to be seen. Even worse, Shelly's given us two demerits each for what would normally be one-demerit offenses—tardiness and speaking out of line. If Annie or I receive one more demerit, we won't be allowed to perform at the football game this Friday.

I guess I'd better swallow down my outrage.

No easy feat.

Shelly proceeds to work us like dogs as we brush up on our "Funkytown" routine.

I used to like that song.

Toward the end of the two hours, we head down to the girls' locker room to change and get ready for second period, and I find myself much calmer, probably due to the good workout. Charlotte and I continue to catch up as we dress; Annie remains in a sad puddle of silence.

Thankfully, she snaps out of it once dressed, and we admire each other in our new back-to-school clothes. It's an unwritten rule: Thou shalt wear new clothes on the first day of school. And I finally have the nerve to ask Annie about what happened to put her on Shelly's bad side.

"All I know is that Shelly left to go to the ladies' room; Rob walked over and started talking to Jeff and me about the football team. Jeff turned around to talk to another friend, and when Shelly came back she went off like a nuclear bomb."

"She's nuts." Charlotte sums up what we're all thinking as we leave to wait out the rest of the period in the gym.

"She's got a screw loose for sure," I can't help but add.

Oh, well. Despite it all, I may actually be happy to be back at school. There's academic pressure and peer pressure and every kind of pressure, but I want to be a glass-half-full kind of girl for once. It may sound silly, but I feel that this year's going to be important.

Even more, for the rest of this week, I'll keep my head down around Shelly. I'm not going to start the year sidelined.

CHAPTER 2

I was six.

"What're you lookin' at?" I sneak up to my sister to spy over her shoulder.

"*Tiger Beat*, of course," Elizabeth responds with indifference and continues to hum away as she flips through the slick pages. We're supposed to be drawing with my new sidewalk chalk, a gift from my grandparents on a recent visit, but I've dropped mine in order to get a better look at what has her so interested.

"Who do you like better: Davy Jones or Bobby Sherman?"

"David Cassidy," she replies on a sigh.

"Yeah, he's cu—" I begin to answer when I hear an echoey noise.

"Help . . . help . . . aaaaah . . . help." It's faint and difficult to hear over the traffic whoosh from Jefferson Street one block over. But it seems to be coming from down the hill that runs along our street.

"Is somebody crying?" I ask her.

"I don't hear anything." She shrugs me off.

But my curiosity has gotten the better of me, and I begin to drift down the block toward the sounds after crouching to pick up a piece of pink chalk, which I clutch tightly in my hand in case of emergency. As I get closer to the corner, the sounds become louder.

"Help! Help me!" There's sobbing and hiccupping. It sounds like a little kid, and it seems to be coming from around the corner and (strangely enough) in the ground.

As I reach the end of the block, I turn onto Cavender Street and realize the person must be inside the storm drain, so I step off the curb in order to stoop down and see what's going on.

All of a sudden, I'm yanked to my feet by my arm and dragged onto the grass. My sister's in my face.

"Lola! Mom's told you not to walk into the street without looking for cars. What were you thinking?" she scolds, but she stops and gets a scrunched-up look on her face as she finally registers the crying.

"What in the world?" she mutters as she becomes distracted, finally drops my arm, looks both ways, and steps off the curb. I rub my arm where she grabbed me; then I follow close behind and bend beside her to look.

And the prettiest little boy I've ever seen is glaring out at us from the storm drain with big, angry eyes the color of a blue jay.

"What took you so long?" he accuses as if we've met before, or we're somehow responsible for his predicament.

I'm not sure how to respond, so I tell him my name, hand him the piece of pink chalk, and tell him we'll go get our mommy.

"Okay, Lowly," he responds with a final hiccup.

The bell signals the end of class, and the drill team begins to file out of the gym.

I push myself up from the floor where we've been waiting out the period and sidle up to Charlotte as we walk to the door.

"Charlotte, pleeeease find the "Funkytown" tape and destroy it for me. I'll be your slave for life." I bat my eyelashes at her for dramatic effect.

Charlotte laughs and rolls her eyes at the same time. This has to be some kind of additional rare talent, along with the eyebrow quirk, and I tell her so.

"You're goofy. See ya later." She gives me a little push of affection in the opposite direction.

"See ya, Charlotte!" I yell over my shoulder as I pivot to scurry down a different hall than the one to which she directed me. It's time for second period, and I need to stop by my locker to drop off some of my school supplies. Once there, I unload my backpack and slam the locker door with a satisfying *thwack!,* giving my padlock an extra, jaunty spin for good measure.

But as I'm about to continue on, I spot a familiar head of dark brown hair hovering above the crowd. It's Earley. I then spy another in close proximity; it's a rare and attractive shade of strawberry-blonde and belongs to my friend Teresa.

They look as if they're deep in conversation. He's stooping to hear her talk over the noise of the hallway, and they both have barley-there smiles on their faces.

And they don't see me, which gives me a shifty idea as I sneak in their direction.

Now they're laughing together, and even though Teresa does spot me, Earley doesn't. Oh, what a wonderfully wondrous opportunity! I motion for Teresa to be quiet; then I make an Olympic-sized leap onto Earley's back, clamping my hands over his eyes. He staggers but manages to stay upright as I ask him to guess at my identity like a moron.

"Lowly, get off me. You almost knocked me down. Practice a little decorum," he sneers, then pushes me off. I land on my feet but overbalance and end up on my bottom.

Yes, if we were counting, this would be my second fall of the day.

I look up. Earley looks halfway amused, halfway concerned; Teresa can't help but laugh.

"Ow," I grimace. "I guess I deserved that."

Earley gives me a hand up, and I dust a surprising amount of school dirt from my bottom. You'd think the new flooring would be cleaner. I try to join in their laughter, but mine sounds anemic, no surprise. My face feels burny and my stomach feels tight, a result of embarrassment and hurt feelings—my actions and Teresa's outright amusement in that order.

I resolve to shake it off and soon recover in order to practice my new goal of self-control; then it's my turn to tease Earley once again.

"'A little decorum?' Our boy is growing up, Teresa; he's using multisyllabic words," I announce.

"I wish *you* would grow up," he mutters.

Then we all crack up.

That's never going to happen.

Earley knows this because he's the closest thing I have to a brother. He lives down the block from me, and we've been friends since his mom, Grace, bought one of the smaller houses in our neighborhood after her divorce from his father. Earley's named after his dad, Howard, almost as unfortunate a name choice as my own. So Earley prefers to be called by his middle name, Grace's maiden name, and we accommodate him for the most part unless he does something too little-brotherish.

"You better be nice," I mock-threaten with narrowed eyes. He looks toward the heavens in response, lets out a longsuffering sigh, and gives my shoulder a resolute squeeze.

Elizabeth and I first discovered him not long after he and Grace moved to our neighborhood. According to Grace, he'd been playing in the backyard but managed to escape his prison despite a locked gate. I heard his cries for help, and we investigated to find he was good and truly stuck in an awkward (and in hindsight, dangerous) way. What if it had rained? It was too deep for him to climb out or for us to pull him out on our own. So we ran for our mother and returned with her just as Grace erupted from their front door in search of her little guy. You see, Earley thought it would be interesting to explore the gutter; then he couldn't get out. If I remember correctly, he was lured into the storm drains by the shine of a copper penny.

Five-year-old boys have an unaccountable sense of adventure.

After we worked out his rescue (Grace had to lie out on the street with her head, shoulders, and arms in the opening while the rest of us cheered her on and watched for cars), we introduced ourselves. Elizabeth and I promptly offered a scratched-up and hysterical little Earley some chalk, which stopped the crying like a charm.

We've been like family ever since.

Over this past summer, Earley has grown at an exponential rate as only adolescent boys can. He's fifteen nearing sixteen and a sophomore but is already over six feet. He's thoughtful, smart, good-looking, and funny, just like Grace, whom I love and admire. I predict I'll be beating off girls with a stick this year, and in fact, I would happily beat up anyone for Earley.

He's my best friend.

"Why were you laughing in church yesterday?" Teresa, whose father is our pastor, pulls me from my reverie.

"Oh, man. Did you hear Mrs. Robbins singing behind us? I know it was wrong to laugh, but her exaggerated vibrato . . . I couldn't stop."

She gives me an amused look and tugs on my sleeve because we're headed to the same class and time's running out; then Pumpkin Evans walks by, and I notice Earley following her with his eyes. Teresa and I greet Pumpkin, a senior, and she stops to respond, her hazel eyes radiating clear and kind despite our need to move on.

She's polite like that.

Earley isn't the only boy who follows Pumpkin with his eyes. She's the most beautiful girl at our school, cheerleading captain, and the epitome of serene. She could be out every night of the week, but her parents won't allow her to date, causing much complaint among the Sunset boys.

Once she leaves, the gleam of her bright auburn hair following behind, Earley says an absent-minded good-bye as he heads off after her, seemingly trailing her glow. I internally sigh, wishing I could be like her—unruffled and serene; then I laugh to myself as I wonder whether Earley's actually going in the right direction for his next class.

Teresa and I look at each other. She smirks. We know we're both thinking the same thing. That's a common occurrence with us.

Except Teresa's next words surprise me. "If she wasn't so nice, it would be a requirement to hate her."

Okay, so we weren't thinking alike. Teresa's normally more careful about her words concerning others, but she's right on the money nevertheless.

I keep that thought to myself. "What do you think about the changes in the school? I think the flooring looks like it belongs in a bathroom." She'll understand my feelings about the remodel.

"I agree. It's horrible. I much preferred the old granite stairwells and the hardwood floors. Those stairwells, they were indented with the history of our school! And what's with the mirrored walls? We'll be tripping over each other trying to get a look at . . ."

Mrs. Smith, our English teacher, tells us to take a seat and then proceeds to reseat us in alphabetical order. On the bright side, this means I'll be sitting by Allen Peters again. Petey's laid-back and doesn't bother me (a real plus in my book), so we quietly say our hellos and settle back into our seats.

Unfortunately, the alphabet is also responsible for my being seated in short shooting distance of the Demented Duo, and I'm suddenly feeling much joy at the year's prospects.

Not.

I turn to say hi to my friend Lauri while handouts are being passed around. She has some tiny, tired smudges beneath her eyes, but she's smiling, a definite relief.

She was diagnosed with leukemia at the beginning of the summer, and she's still undergoing treatment. For some reason, we don't talk about the details among our group of friends. We act as if everything's normal. My parents tell me she's doing fine. They get their information from her parents. But as a result of her treatment, she's returned to school with a light-brown wig that she'll be wearing while her own hair grows out.

The wig is pretty.

Or maybe she makes the wig pretty.

Neither the disease nor the hair loss has slowed down her wit, incidentally.

She leans over and whispers, "Lola, it's a little scary, but Matthew's starting to look like Harrison Ford—a slightly dirty Harrison Ford, but Harrison Ford nonetheless. What do you think?"

"I can't get past the smell. And what's with the beer t-shirt?" We both grin like maniacs at our droll observations about half of the Duo as Mrs. Smith continues to hand out copies of the Junior Honors English syllabus.

Fortunately, before Matthew and Luke have a chance to notice me and get in any digs, Mrs. Smith begins class by going over the syllabus. But when she leaves the class about halfway through the period to make a few extra copies of another handout to distribute, they get their chance.

"Lola! Get any this summer, tease? I hope somebody loosened you up for the rest of us," Matthew announces for the whole class. Luke's face is scrunched up in some ridiculous expression as he snickers away as if this is the funniest thing he's ever heard.

The school year has hardly started, and they've already reduced me to a dirty object. My shoulders tense up. I put my hands over my eyes, maybe in a futile desire to hide from their words or deny the truth of their existence. They don't bother me, I tell myself. Then I realize I've stopped breathing. Almost involuntarily, I turn and give them our drill team captain's Medusa glare, but it doesn't seem to be as effective when I use it.

Crap.

But I'm not the dirty object. They are.

"I see neither of you tapeworms grew a conscience or cultivated a decent sense of humor over the summer. You're disgusting."

"Who's joking? You wouldn't think it was so disgusting if you had a few minutes alone with me," Matthew carries on with a slimy leer, adding what I'm guessing is a foul name for me that I've never heard before. I'll have to ask Charlotte if she knows its meaning later.

"That offer holds no temptation for me, coming from an invertebrate and all." I hear some subdued laughter from the direction of Petey, Lauri, and even Luke (that's a surprise.) in response; then Mrs. Smith reenters the room. She seems to be a bit hard of hearing, because like so many of our teachers in the past, she's not inclined to overhear the waste Matthew and Luke disgorge or my responses.

It would be worth getting in trouble every now and then to have an adult actually stand up to the perverts.

"Blah, blah, blah, blah, blah." She begins her lesson, and like the grownups in Charlie Brown, not much of what she has to say is worth our full attention.

My mind drifts back to my two archenemies seated a few closely spaced chairs away. Matthew (like Earley, but a year later) has grown tremendously in height over the past year; Luke hasn't.

Despite Matthew's need for a good haircut, the aforementioned beer shirt, and his oftentimes mean personality, he is starting to look grown-up, and rather handsome as Lauri mentioned.

This makes me want to puke a little bit.

The Demented Duo are always together. They're close neighbors to each other, a twisted parallel to Earley and me. Furthermore and despite today's example, they're way too smart for their own or anyone else's good. They're nipping at my heels for class rank without even trying. It's inexplicable, but they're popular too. Though I often accuse them of having no decent sense of humor, in reality, they can be funny if their put-downs aren't directed at you. I have to admit that sometimes I can't help laughing at their sarcasm even if it will always be against my better judgment.

But I fire at them more often than I laugh. Much more often. Thanks to them, I'm not sure I'll ever get my temper under control.

Right as I'm done mulling the whole awful situation over, Luke lets out a prime example.

"Steve. You're looking good. Not. When was the last time you brushed your hair?"

As if he should be talking. Poor Steve, often a target due to his neglected appearance and Coke-bottle glasses, swipes a sheepish hand across the top of his head and shrugs, probably hoping the bell will soon ring. The irony is that Steve is one of Matthew and Luke's so-called friends.

Unbelievable.

The bell rings, signaling the end of the period. As we gather our belongings in preparation to exit the classroom, Matthew bumps me with his shoulder, causing me to drop a pencil. Petey stoops to pick it up for me; then I look up to catch Matthew giving me a glare that would freeze water before stalking away.

I may pay for having the last word.

CHAPTER 3

Lauri, Teresa, and I gather across the hall from the choir room.

I'm not looking forward to seeing Mr. Atwood, the choir director. I enjoy his class, but I have a strong suspicion he doesn't like me much. Actually, he's probably just one of the myriad of people who think I'm conceited. (Unlike my other character defects, that criticism *has* reached my ears.)

I don't think it's true. I'm rather shy until I get to know a person; then you can't pry me loose. Anyway, I've found people often mistake my shyness for a stuck-up attitude. It's hard for me to understand, but it's something I've learned to live with and ignore for the most part. Or maybe I'm deluding myself, and I am a bit conceited. But I'm not sure I feel like self-critique at this moment, so I'll have to think about it later.

Working on my self-control gives me enough to think about.

While I get a sip of water out of something that looks like a spaceship, Lauri and Teresa end their conversation and move to enter the class. I follow close behind them and notice Thomas Florence hovering at the door. He's bouncing on his heels as if in anticipation of Christmas. His tight, light blond curls reflect his energy.

This is not good.

Thomas, with whom I used to be on fairly friendly terms, seems to have a not-so-secret crush on me. I like him just fine when he's not staring at me. I truly admire him as a musician (he plays some beautiful guitar), and he's not bad looking. However, the overt way he expresses his admiration makes me extremely uncomfortable.

Besides, I hate to admit this, but I'm not confident enough to date a guy who's shorter than me.

"Hey there, ladies," Thomas says in what he thinks is a smooth voice and then has the audacity to wink at me. He's gained some unexpected confidence over the summer.

Lauri snickers; I'm back with my buddy, Humiliation; and Teresa, ever gracious, answers for the three of us. "Hi, Thomas," she responds as we shuffle in the door.

Lauri and I part with Teresa at the soprano section, the closest one to the entrance; Teresa heads over to sit with the altos. I find a seat by Annie. Lauri sits on my other side, and the three of us continue to converse quietly while waiting for the start of class.

Thomas follows us in and lingers around the piano at the front of the room. A guitar, probably his, is perched on top. I wonder why he's not sitting down with the other tenors but quickly put it out of my mind. Mr. Atwood will direct Thomas to the proper section once he decides to grace us with his presence, and when I say "grace us with his presence," I'm not kidding.

Like magic, the choir director materializes just outside the door with another teacher before he pulls it closed, remaining in the hall. He then proceeds to have a conversation even though the bell for class has already rung. We hear them talk and laugh and talk and chuckle as we sit around and chat.

I'm wondering which student the two teachers are discussing.

Thomas sits down at a stool by the piano, pulls over his guitar, and starts to play a subdued tune, most likely of his own composing.

The door sways open, and Mr. Adonis (I mean Atwood) strides into the room with his customary flair, arrives at the piano, and claps his hands twice for attention even though he's already gained it with his looks alone.

The man embodies the Greek god.

Again, I'm not kidding.

"Listen. Welcome to a new school year. I hope you had a fabulous summer. I know *I* did. Unfortunately for moi, we're stuck together for the next several months, so let's make the most of it . . . blah, blah, blah." His silky voice is so pleasant one could almost ignore the insults.

Mr. Atwood actually says "blah, blah, blah," by the way. I didn't make it up this time.

Then to my surprise, he motions to Thomas, and instead of demanding Thomas vacate the piano bench, starting to hand out music, or belittling us longer, Mr. Atwood speaks again.

"Thomas has asked to play and sing a song he composed over the summer; I've granted him permission to perform it for the class this morning."

Mr. Atwood turns toward a nearby chair to sit facing the front. Half the girls in the class emit small sighs as his magnificence is veiled once more. They can breathe again.

His appearance, however, soon drops into insignificance, at least for me.

As the choir director strikes an artful yet unstudied pose in his chair, Thomas begins to play his composition. It begins with lovely, melodic chord progressions, but then he regrettably begins to sing.

It's not his singing voice that's the problem.

It's the lyrics.

This could well be one of the biggest nightmares of my high school career.

I love the way you move and smile at me.
I know you're shy, but I can see,
Through all the things that put false barriers between us.
Lovely Lola, you're beautiful.

All at once, I no longer hear the words.

I may be having my first ever out-of-body experience.

This can't be happening.

I look around to the horrifying discovery that instead of the class facing the front of the room and watching Thomas, they seem to be fixated on *me*. Some of them have the deer-caught-in-headlights look, some of them look as if they're about to explode with laughter (their red faces and puffy cheeks indicate their struggle to hold it in), and some of them look almost as embarrassed as I am.

On instinct, I try to scrunch down in my chair as far as possible. The heat rushes to my face for the millionth time today, and I close my eyes.

This song can't possibly be about me.

It just can't.

I crack open one eye to see Thomas continue to happily and sappily sing away while shooting looks in my direction, obviously oblivious to the class's reaction. I crack open my other eye, but all faces are still pretty much glued on me. Grasping for denial with all my might, I close my eyes once again and do an internal chant. It's not about me, it's not about me, he's not singing about me. He is *not* singing about and to me in front of almost fifty other teenagers. Considering our junior class has around 375 members, fifty is a fairly large percentage of the school population.

The song *finally* over, Thomas stands up and beams at me, but I quickly look away. Mr. Atwood contributes his usual subdued clapping, and the rest of the class joins in, albeit with reluctance. I can't even gather up the nerve to give a halfhearted grimace. My best defense at this point is to pretend ignorance if I'm able. Anyway, I'm sure it's a coincidence that he used my name in the song. After all, it rhymes with so many things like . . . um . . . cola. Well, actually, I can't think of any at the moment, but I'm sure it does. And how does he even remember my smile as he insinuates with those lyrics? It's been over six months since he's seen it, due to his unwanted attention. If he really knew me, he'd run for the hills.

He'd better start running now.

Mr. Atwood soon realizes the student clapping has stopped, so he ceases. Thank goodness! He asks Thomas to take a seat with smiles and fondness, causing my sourness to escalate, and starts grabbing stacks of music to pass out, all the while chatting about the school year ahead. We then get started on the real business of being in choir: singing.

It's about time.

I continue to slouch in my seat and try to focus on my music. Maybe if I pretend nothing happened, everyone else will go along with it. Although I have to admit singing is a bit difficult while slouching, it's not stopping me from trying to become one with my chair.

As we're putting away our music, Lauri leans over, her hair brushing my cheek, and in an audible whisper says, "Well, Lola. What did you think about Thomas's song?"

"Kill me now," I groan.

Annie hears her question and my response and starts to snicker. This irritates me further, so I send her a look. Lauri's been very sick. I'll gift her a little grace, but as for Annie . . .

"What did *I* do?" she asks with a confused, offended expression. An eye roll comprises my whole response. Maybe after much time has passed, like a jillion-trillion years or so, I'll find this funny. But at present, it's only fed my mortification and barely controlled temper on the first day of school.

Then I realize I should've sprinted out the door as soon as the bell rang.

Thomas is hovering right outside.

I'm losing it.

As I follow my friends from the classroom, I keep my eyes glued to the ground and try to stick with them as closely as possible.

It doesn't work.

"Did you like it, Lola?" He addresses me with mind-boggling directness instead of letting me go my way. He looks so normal and hopeful.

That's the last straw!

"No, I didn't *like* it! Why couldn't you have just written me some bad poetry, and plastered it all over the billboard across the street from the school? At least it would've been a little more *anonymous!*" I hear someone screech and realize it's me.

His face morphs into a confused and hurt mess, causing *me* confusion over my reaction.

I can't process this.

And I don't know how to fix it.

"Nice, Lola." Andrew Walker, the senior class vice president, comments over his shoulder. He must've heard my outburst as he passed by.

I then notice all my friends have left me.

"Aargh!" I stomp my foot and turn back to Thomas. He's regained his composure enough to give me a look somewhere between scared and angry; then he turns to stalk away.

My paralysis is broken when I realize I have two minutes to get to my next class. I rush toward it; then I abruptly stop in the middle of the hallway. My thoughts are swirling and swilling around my head like the students bypassing me as if I'm a rock in the middle of a river. I know I don't have much time, but I'm overwhelmed by how out of control this day has become. It's painfully obvious that my goal of self-control needs to be extended to everyone and not just the Demented Duo.

I think I need a nap . . . or chocolate.

Unfortunately, that's not in the cards for me at present.

I take a deep breath and remove myself as an obstacle to the student body. As I begin my movement, I merge back into the flow

of people and say a quick prayer that the rest of the day will hold less drama.
God, show me what to do.
I hope my mom is praying too.

CHAPTER 4

It's the second day of school, and as I meander through the hall toward the cafeteria, I see George the Gorgeous with his girlfriend and a group of her friends. George calls out to me, so I stop to catch up with him. His girlfriend, Michelle, stays for a moment to whisper in his ear, gives me a malevolent glare (which she is careful to hide from George), says an anemic hello, and continues on her way, cheerleader friends in tow.

"Your face is in a grimace. Why does your smile look as if you're in pain whenever you see Michelle?" His eyes have narrowed, but they hold a glint of amusement as if he might guess the answer.

"Oh, no. You think so? You must be misreading me." I look everywhere but at him as I answer with a tiny shake of my head.

"Uh-huh." His voice holds traces of skepticism.

George is a senior this year and student body president. He's on the football team and the baseball team, in the National Honor Society, and involved in any number of other activities. Yes, you've guessed it—George is our BMOC (Big Man on Campus). He seems to take all the activity and attention in stride or even thrive on it, as if it's as natural a part of life as a heartbeat. Despite this or maybe because of it, he's surprisingly friendly and down to earth.

To myself I call him George the Gorgeous because I've had a crush on him for the last year and more. He's six feet and a bit, with silky, sandy blond hair, friendly blue eyes, and a walk that says he owns the hallways. He has a sharp sense of humor not unlike Lauri's. It doesn't happen very often because I'm too much in awe of him, but once I relax around him enough to breathe, we can laugh and joke together just like old friends.

Which is what we are.

We're as old friends as sixteen- and seventeen-year-olds can be. George was a common fixture in my life when I was little. He and his parents attended my church when we were babies, and we frequently played at each other's houses during our preschool years.

If our rekindled friendship continues to progress, he could grow to be like a brother to me, like Earley, but I've been crushing on him for way too long. Not that he's ever noticed.

He leans down to whisper in my ear, "Lola, whatever is going on with you and Michelle, you have my permission to ignore it." His close proximity causes my eyes to bug out and my face to become prickly. The hallway feels ten degrees warmer.

I compose myself as he straightens up and give him a lopsided nod while keeping my eyes on the floor. I'm not sure how to respond. I'm far from ready to admit any issue with his girlfriend. But George is always right, in my brief experience, so I guess I'll take his advice.

Do I idealize him? Yes.

His family left our church to attend another nearby when George and I were about six and five. Our families grew distant despite living only a few blocks apart and attending the same schools.

This left a bit of a gap in my life and my sister's too, but I guess God realized Elizabeth and I needed another boy to play with us, because Earley showed up to fill in the hole left by George about six months later.

It amazes me that I'm beginning to know George again after all these years.

We continue to discuss the latest news as we head toward the cafeteria, but I stop to buy some candy and a Tab at the snack counter just outside. He goes on to catch up with Michelle.

I used to like Michelle. She's a super friendly, happy, cute girl until she catches sight of me. It turns out I made a fatal mistake one day when my mom was asked to give George a ride home. I saw him in the car, and in my excitement to spend time with him, I hopped in the back seat with him to chat instead of the front seat with her. Several students were milling around the parking lot to witness my misstep. I didn't even think about how it looked, which was rather dorky of me, and in retrospect, beaucoup embarrassing.

Charlotte later let me know she heard through the grapevine that Michelle saw me get into the back seat and was furious. I'm not sure what Michelle thought we'd get up to with my mom driving, but she's disliked me ever since.

Is Michelle insecure? Obviously. The why is none of my business, but she'll never see me go after George. She'll never see me go after anyone. That's neither my style nor my confidence level. I'm not Shelly, our supreme queen drill team captain. George, as is the case with many of the boys I find handsome, is out of my league. I feel privileged that he stops and talks to me every now and then. That's all I can expect.

I pay for my much-needed chocolate and caffeine treasure, grab it from where it's been placed on the smooth glass countertop, and hurry to catch up with my friends.

I step into the cafeteria, and all the conflicting feelings of the place converge upon me. The cafeteria is its own amazing wonderland of teenage contradiction wrapped up in the center of the basement level of the school, glaringly lit with fluorescence, garishly painted, complete with Formica-topped tables paired with purple plastic chairs.

There are no windows.

What's the contradiction? On the one hand, you have the social aspect of the cafeteria. Freedom. It's the one time during the day when we're free to sit where we want (with friends), free to eat what we want (within limits), and free to say what we think (with relief). On the other hand, its physical atmosphere is stuffy, holds too many teenagers, smells of fried food, and lacks cleanliness. Funkytown.

It would not be anyone's first choice of place to spend their prized downtime, but it's all we've got at Sunset other than the pecan grove where the smokers congregate out back.

I scan the room for my friends and note a few surprising additions to our usual cafeteria crowd. Strangely enough, Pumpkin—her auburn hair lighting the way as a beacon—and Jack, a senior friend from church, have decided to join the rest of our usual gang, consisting of Earley, Teresa, Charlotte, Lauri, Annie, and Jeff, Annie's on-again, off-again boyfriend.

As I plop my bounty down at an empty seat between Charlotte and Earley, I wonder why Jack and Pumpkin would be joining us for lunch. I guess I'm too hungry to puzzle it out at present, because nothing comes to mind. So I put myself in my seat and tear into my M&Ms; then I pop the top on my Tab.

Ahhhh. I love that sound.

I chew my chocolate goodness, and the brain cells start working again. My thoughts turn toward Jack, whom I've known for several years. Because I'm a year younger and we aren't in the same electives, our paths don't often cross at school. But as I mentioned, we attend the same church, and I consider him a friend. Although some might characterize him as the stereotypical band nerd, Jack's one of the kindest people I know. He's consistently nice. That's a huge character bonus in my opinion. One is pretty safe with Jack.

Jack's best friend, David, graduated last year. Maybe *that's* why he's chosen to sit with us during lunch.

As to why Pumpkin is at our table instead of with Michelle and George at the cheerleader table, I have no idea.

I continue to eat and begin to tune in my ears to the conversations surrounding me. Earley's brilliance strikes.

"Hmm. Let's see what you're eating, Teresa," he archly exclaims. Teresa beams and holds up her brown paper lunch bag by the bottom to spill its contents onto the table. She's already removed her chicken salad on white (her mother makes the best in the world), but out rolls an apple and a Ding Dong as well.

She happily pokes around at her food as Earley gifts us with his insight into the hidden messages of her lunch.

"I think your sandwich and apple indicate the steadiness and stability of your character, while the Ding Dong graces us with a glimpse into your ability to easily discern the characters of others . . . with a dollop of sincere sweetness thrown in."

Jack snorts but quickly tries to hide it with a cough.

Teresa continues to glow.

Pumpkin smiles beatifically.

Pumpkin *always* smiles beatifically.

I think Earley catches Jack's snort, because he turns his laser beams on him next.

"So, Jack, my friend. What are you eating today?"

Jack, who purchased his lunch, shrugs and points to his tray. "I've got chicken-fried steak, mashed potatoes, green beans, and some chocolate cake. What're you gonna make of that?"

Earley responds with a confident grin as we wait for his reply. "You hide your deep care for others and your Star Trek obsession under the trappings of understated but intelligent wit. You're easily satisfied with what's on your metaphorical plate, unlike so many. In other words, when you do complain or become self-effacing, it's to deflect and change a subject or situation you find uncomfortable."

"Here's your five cents, Lucy. Keep your day job," Jack snickers as he flicks Earley a nickel previously forgotten on his tray. The rest of us burst into laughter as Earley catches the coin, smiles with good humor, and twists to face me.

Uh-oh. Here it comes. Earley, whose grin has become fiendish, will want to get me back for the teasing I dished out before second period yesterday. Or maybe he'll put on his brother hat and chastise me for the lack of nutritional content in my lunch. Or maybe both.

"Lola. My dear, dear *sister*, Lola. I think we can all see what you're eating. No surprise there."

"Hey, li'l bro." I toast him with my Tab can and consider a quick exit from the room. I need to throw away my candy wrapper, right? In fact, some fresh air is sounding pretty good right now, even if the only place to get it is in the smoker's grove outside.

"Some M&Ms and a Tab," he states.

"They're peanut M&Ms," I reply with hope.

He gives me a long look and graciously corrects himself. "Okay. Lola has some *peanut* M&Ms and a Tab. This is going to be pretty easy, I think."

I'm not feeling good about this.

"The nature of your lunch indicates a desire for a quick albeit insufficient fix. A wish to feel comfort and obtain energy quickly despite knowing that it's not good for you in the long run. In fact, forget about the long run; you'll probably hit a sugar low within the next hour while you need to focus in class. The lack of any real substance may also indicate a lack of substance in your character. You're easily distracted by the pretty and transient. You're whimsical, charming, and I'll even admit, cute—after all, it runs in the *family*—but are often self-absorbed or lost in your own head. And your mouth and temper are out-of—"

I thought Thomas's performance yesterday was the worst moment of my high school career.

I was wrong.

Instead, Earley's words seem ten times worse. Earley, whom I love with all my heart, is cutting, and cutting, and cutting into me.

My spirit sinks like a mob victim in the Hudson River, fitted with concrete shoes.

I feel my body start to slump; my face begin to burn. My mouth takes an involuntary downturn. Then my eyes start to water. I look around briefly, frantically, and notice everyone is staring at us with O-shaped mouths as he unheedingly continues to prattle.

No! I refuse to cry in the cafeteria. With what feels like an inhuman effort, I swipe my eyes and shove down the hurt with a resolve I didn't know I possessed. But I guess some emotion has to come out somehow.

Anger sees her opening and explodes with a force.

"How can you *say* these things to me?" I grit out toward the table as I shoot out of my chair and back away.

But anger likes company. I wish I could remember that. Earley's mouth sets itself in a stubborn slash. "How could you say those things to Thomas yesterday? I heard what you said, Lola. It was brutal. And I'm probably the only one who cares enough about you to confront you." The beautiful blue of his eyes is hidden within confrontational slits.

"You dare to say this is care? Maybe you should give me the benefit of the doubt. Maybe you should ask my side of the story. *Maybe* you should've waited to talk to me about this in *private! Thanks* for ruining my lunch!" My voice escalates. I know I should've controlled my frustration with Thomas yesterday, but Earley has another think coming if he thinks this is the way to get me to fix that situation.

"What lunch?" Earley hisses under his breath.

I kick my chair, sending it crashing back under the table, and grab my lunch trash with shaking hands as I turn to get away. My Tab can gives a satisfying crunching noise as I crush it in my grip. I hear Charlotte call after me and momentarily turn back to the table to see Earley looking unrepentant and Charlotte radiating concern. Even Pumpkin looks a little shaken up. Her perfectly tweezed auburn eyebrows are hidden in her bangs. But I continue on out the door.

Then I notice the whole cafeteria is as quiet as the dead.

I wish I was better at hiding my feelings, but at least I'm not crying.

If I had a cigarette, moreover, I wouldn't just be sharing the pecan grove with the smokers right now.

Escape is paramount.

CHAPTER 5

I was in preschool and George was in kindergarten.

I think about this memory a lot lately.

Georgie and me are sitting in the large group area of Williamson's waiting for one of our mommies to pick us up. As we wait, the other kids begin to trickle out one or two at a time as their parents come to get them.

When we're down to around four other kids, I realize we've never been picked up this late, and I begin to feel confused.

We continue to perch on a stair that leads up to a stage used during group time. We're now the only two left in the room. Teachers and other grownups breeze in and out to check on us, then continue on with their end-of-day tasks.

A light bulb goes off in my head, and I gasp.

No one is coming for us!

My body goes stiff as a statue.

I can't breathe right.

"H-H-How w-will we g-get ho-home?" I stutter out to Georgie as tears begin to slide down my face. I hear myself make little hiccupping noises. My mommy says this is because I've gulped in too much air.

"It's okay, Lola. This has happened to me before, and they always end up coming. It's okay. We can play Batman when we get home. I bet Elizabeth will let you be Batgirl this time." He soothes me with his voice and small pats on the back with his chubby hand.

This calms me because Georgie knows everything.

I end up crying anyway.

George, of all people, finds me crouched in a nook under the stairs with my fists covering my eyes.

"Lola, come out of there. I know I'll hit my head if I try to pull you out."

I consider staying in my hiding place—I'm sure my face is blotchy with tears and not-well-repressed emotion—but this is George, so I feel myself creeping out almost against my will.

I wonder if he still knows everything.

"Wow. I didn't think one person's face could get so many shades of pink and red," he says while rubbing the back of his neck. "You made quite a scene in there, bobcat."

I just nod my head up and down; my chin is trembling, and I don't think I should talk.

"You know what? I'm glad you can take up for yourself. I think you've got a lot of spirit, Lola. That was a little scary, but . . ."

"I'm sorry, George, but this has been the second of two of the worst days of my life," I eke out.

"Don't apologize to me. Now, from what I hear, you may need to apologize to Thomas. And I don't know what's up with Earley lately. I may start calling him Surly Earley if he doesn't get a better attitude. Or I may give him a slight pounding if he doesn't treat you better. Better yet, we'll ask Thomas to write an ode to Earley's moodiness and sing it to him out on the practice field. Then he might be a little more understanding."

This makes me laugh despite myself.

French class has ended; it feels like a miracle that I'm headed to the last class of the day. Of the second longest day of my high school career.

Mr. Graham teaches trigonometry, and he's a bit eccentric for a teacher. Despite the fact he's required to use them, Mr. Graham, with his slight East European accent (or something like that), doesn't believe in seating charts or grades or anything very conventional.

He's kind and patient but has an odd sense of humor. Every now and then, he resorts to calling us names. Not bad names per se, but names nonetheless. Teasing us. He mostly directs the names at the girls in his classes, calling us prima donnas. We didn't know what it meant at first but looked it up. Of course. Not so flattering, but I guess he considers us slightly full of ourselves, and in all honesty, we may be. Our lone possible defense is that it's pretty darn difficult to find people who aren't self-absorbed and don't think the world revolves around them. So I guess the only real strike against Mr. Graham's behavior is that the boys seem to be exempt.

He begins class in his rather plodding, ponderous voice; I try to concentrate, but I sit by an open window.

The silvery-chipped radiator is on my right, next comes the beige-painted sill, and then the warmth and wide openness. The sun, clear sky, and green trees are calling my name; their leaves rustle-rustle in the breeze. Some boys jog around the practice field; from my second-story vantage point, I have a spectacular view.

They're beautiful, those boys.

They have long, muscular, lean legs in varying shades of brown to tan that move with grace and speed. I'm wondering if the boys feel free and unleashed as they zoom around the track, or if it feels like a chore, just another practice.

Then I notice Earley among them, and my chest starts to tighten up a bit.

I have incentive to turn away from the window and tune in to Mr. Graham. He's passing out a worksheet.

I need to concentrate on class after all.

As Mr. Graham passes me my paper, he pauses to focus on me.

"How was your summer, Lola? I did not get to ask you yesterday."

"Just great, Mr. Graham," I reply, but thinking about my good summer reminds me how incredibly sour the past few days have been. I can still see that glimpse of Earley even though I'm no longer looking. All of a sudden, my stomach has a boulder in it.

I take a deep breath, release it, and try to regain some control.

Mr. Graham must notice my sigh, because he pats me on the shoulder as he passes to return to his desk and start his lecture.

"Class, please turn to page 5 in your textbook. We will begin today with some basic definitions. I will then describe your assignment. It is not too difficult, and you should easily be able to complete it in class. Do not expect that to be the case on most days. Trigonometry is a challenging class. If you are not up to a challenge, you should not be in here," he continues on, and I do my best to be "up to the challenge."

Did I mention Mr. Graham does not use contractions? For better or worse, the same can't be said of me.

We start our work, and he steps out to grab some coffee, or papers, or whatever reason teachers step out of the room. Maybe they need a quiet moment.

A sultry breeze, light traffic sounds, coaches' whistles, and sundry team noises continue to filter into the open window. But I would rather have as little homework as possible, so with forced diligence, I focus on my worksheet for once instead of the many distractions this world offers.

Matthew and Luke, however, have already zoomed through their problems like the near geniuses they are. Now it's time for them to sit like sweet angels and read a book or something else incredibly quiet and kitten-like. Not.

They turn on a poor soul seated on their side of the room. His name is Sam Lancaster, and I've known him since first grade. He's a nice, respectful guy, but I wouldn't characterize him as shy.

Matthew and Luke have teased him for years about some too-short jeans he wore in seventh grade.

"Hey, high-water!" Matthew shouts; then he proceeds to kick Sam's chair. The berating continues from there. Sam tries to ignore them, but it's hard to ignore the chair kicking and curse-word slinging now at play.

I try to turn my attention back on my work, but with the disruption they're creating it's almost impossible.

Then they start pushing on Sam's head and making rude suggestions about his manhood. My irritation mounts as I realize I'm not going to be able to concentrate to finish my assignment. Shouldn't I come to Sam's rescue? Then I remember that Earley tells me if I take up for a guy, it makes the guy look even weaker. I don't understand this, but he usually gives me good advice, so even though he's torn out my heart and stomped on it, I guess I should listen, especially if Sam wouldn't welcome my interference.

Nope! They've moved on to insults of Sam's mother. Forget Earley—I've had it with him *and* the Demented Duo.

"Hey! Could you shut up over there, you moronic monkey bottoms? I don't know about everyone else, but I would like to get my work done. And leave Sam's mom alone while you're at it."

Wow. I've impressed even myself. That inventive name-calling was way better than an expletive. Maybe my mom was right.

Like perfectly timed automatons, their heads swivel toward me. Then Matthew stands up.

"Sure, Lola," he replies in an emotionless voice, "anything you say, ___." Unlike yesterday, insert expletive with which I've the misfortune to be too familiar. "We can talk about your grandmother instead. I've heard she was so—"

I don't let him finish. "I've had it with you and the trash you spew. I'm warning you now, I'm getting you kicked out of this school somehow, someway." I growl as I stand up and begin to walk toward his side of the room. I know in all likelihood it's an impotent threat, but I mean it with every fiber of my being.

Then Mr. Graham walks back into the room, and I redirect my body toward the pencil sharpener; Matthew sits down. Thank goodness Mr. Graham doesn't question my roundabout route. Luckily, I didn't put my pencil down when I stood up. Maybe my subconscious was hoping to stab Matthew with it.

Or maybe I knew I'd need a way to escape.

I don't know how the Duo manage it, but the abuse seems to multiply in their case. One plus one does not equal two in the case of Matthew and Luke. It equals enough persecution for up to four at a time.

Of course, Sam doesn't thank me.

Time moves; the last bell finally rings.

Charlotte has promised to drive me home, and I plan on meeting her in the parking lot. I swing by my locker to drop off my books and then zip, zig, and zag around the other students toward escape.

But just as I'm free of the school doors, and they're clanging shut behind me, I hear a voice I almost always welcome calling my name—Earley's. At present, however, I feel the need to hurry away from the voice. I ignore the call and pick up my pace after my instinctive pause.

I see Charlotte's bright red VW Bug and sprint in its direction, but just as I reach the edge of the parking lot, I pull up short. Earley will be riding home with her too. Drat. It was stupid to forget our normal routine. I guess there's no escape, so I slow my pace. I hear his footsteps respond to mine; he's no longer running, but I don't turn around.

I keep walking.

As I near the car, I note Charlotte's already sitting in it.

I turn with reluctance to face him. There's no getting out of this confrontation.

With his hands held up in a gesture of almost-surrender, Earley approaches me and begins to speak. "Lola, I know you don't want to talk to me right now, but I want to apologize for what happened in the cafeteria. If you'll give me time to explain—"

My eyes start to water; the tears and his words combine to make me angry.

"You've got to be kidding me. An excuse? Why the change of heart? Oh, I understand now. George talked to you." My voice is too loud. I don't even know why I'm yelling.

But anger loves company.

"Just *listen!*" he shouts. He rarely raises his voice, so this gets my attention, but not in a good way.

I stomp my foot like a small child in response. I'm frustrated, and I have no more words. I look down at the ground then back at the car to see Charlotte emerge from it.

"Calm down, you two," she gently chastises.

"She won't listen, Charlotte!" he exclaims.

I clear my throat and ask him to continue with an imperious wave of my hand.

"I know you're mad at me, but I was trying to say that I don't want to hash this out in the school parking lot. Can I come by your house after dinner tonight? I knew you were upset, so I asked George to give me a ride home, but I need to talk to you."

I nod my head yes, but it seems my lips have decided to wear a sardonic smirk.

"I'm sorry," he mouths and turns to walk toward George's car, shoulders slumped, a fully illustrated picture of dejection.

In fact, he looks so pathetic I'm inclined to forgive him now without having heard his side of the story. But only for a moment.

He doesn't look that pathetic.

Because how can I be a light if his words snuff me out? He called me shallow. Self-absorbed. Everything I'm striving not to be.

He called me out of control.

In front of everyone.

Charlotte and I climb into her car and pull the red doors shut with a subtle creak. I crank down the window, close my eyes, and melt into the seat with an audible sigh as I wait for Charlotte to start up the car. But I don't hear the key turn over, so I glance over to see what she's doing.

She's looking at me with some kind of funny, accepting smile on her face; it's the kind of sympathetic smile only Charlotte can make.

I can't help it; I give her a little smile back.

She's a good friend.

"I heard you've had a few bad days. What happened?"

"Did you hear about Thomas in choir yesterday? I didn't get a chance to talk to you about it."

"Um . . . I did!" she replies with her deep chuckle; then her little nose and mouth wrinkle up in a grimace. And even though I still don't think it's funny, I can't help but laugh as well. Actually, I think my body is trying to relieve some tension, and it's coming out as laughter.

I guess it's better than crying.

"Sorry for laughin', Lola, but you have to admit, it's *funny,*" she asserts. Then, all of a sudden, she takes a deep breath and sobers up.

"Anything else you want to share, other than the thing that happened with Earley at lunch?"

"Only the usual stuff. Matthew and Luke were good and truly wretched in English yesterday, and trig today. I hate it, but I guess it's to be expected."

"'Truly wretched,' were they? I think you've been readin' too much *Anne of Green Gables* again." I huff out a partial chuckle in response.

"*So*—not only has Earley hurt your feelings, but Thomas has embarrassed you, and Matthew and Luke, well, have behaved like Matthew and Luke normally do."

She starts up the car and proceeds to pull out of the parking lot.

"That pretty much sums it up. You know, Charlotte, I don't understand what I've done to those two for them to target me the way they have." I turn to look at her. Her blonde hair is blowing around in the breeze created by the open windows; a piece of hair gets stuck in her mouth. She's shifting gears, so she daintily, impatiently spits it out before continuing.

"Oh, come on! You don't have to do anything with those two. They're twisted. Matthew vomits it out, and Luke is along for the ride. It might diffuse them a bit if you ignored them, but I'm not sure you're that kind of girl. Seriously, I think they enjoy rilin' you up."

I groan because I'm sure she's right.

"Not only that, but . . . do you think Matthew might have a crush on you?"

"Are you kidding me? He *hates* me. End of story. Anyway, I don't think they have the word 'crush' in their vocabulary—it's too innocent."

I don't want to talk about this. "So can we change the subject now?" I beg.

"Sure, but now I need to talk to you about Earley. I know his little lunchtime stunt bothered you." She makes air quotes with one hand as she says the word *bothered*. "But you can't let him get to you like that. He was completely wrong, but your reaction was over the top. I looked at you as he was talking and could tell you'd entered into that volcanic place in your head. You know, the place where the pressure builds and builds?"

Yeah, I do know it. I hate it. I don't know how to stop it.

Or maybe I don't hate it, and that's the whole problem.

As she's speaking we pull up to my house.

"You have much homework tonight? You want to come in for a while?" I ask.

"No and yes." I like the succinctness of her answer.

We get out of the car, grab our bags, and slam the doors in unison.

"I don't think my mom's home. I think she had classes this afternoon," I tell Charlotte. Mom is going back to real estate school, so she can get her license to sell houses. With Elizabeth in college, my parents say we need the extra income.

I turn the key in the lock and push the door open to discover by the pile of mail strewn over our tiny entryway that I was right. Mom's not home. I step over the stack and bend down to pick it up, clearing a path for Charlotte. I don't want her to trip over it as she follows me into the house.

"I'm starving. You want something to eat?" I ask.

"Sure! It's been a long day." She sighs.

We rummage around in the cabinets, decide on some cereal, and sit ourselves down at the canary-yellow breakfast bar to forget our troubles in some crunchy goodness.

Suddenly Charlotte gets a serious look on her face. A little difficult with a mouth full of dry cereal, but she manages it.

"Listen, Lola. I'm going to let Earley deal with what he said at lunch. He's coming over later, right? But I may have an idea about why he lashed out like that."

I tense up. I'm not sure I'm ready to hear this, because it sounds like another criticism is coming my way.

I take a deep breath and determine not to be defensive, no easy feat for me.

"Okay. What did I do?" I say with resignation and freeze as if for a blow.

"You didn't do anything wrong," Charlotte states with emphasis, "but I think Earley wants to assert his, um, I guess you could say grown-upness more. When you persist in referring to him as your little brother, I think he sees it as a put-down."

No way, I think as I start to protest (so much for not being defensive), but before I can get a word out Charlotte continues.

"Wait. Let me finish," she responds with a petite eye roll, "I know you care about Earley. We all care about him. He's a terrific guy, but he's not perfect, and he's sometimes, surprisingly, a bit insecure. I think you should lay off the little brother talk for a bit."

"Maybe, Charlotte, but I do think of him as my little brother. Is that a bad thing? I don't think so."

"It's not that, it's just . . ."

"Whatever his reasoning," I go on, waving my spoon, "he shouldn't have done that at lunch. Still, I can try to stop the brother stuff if it makes him feel belittled." I stuff another spoonful of cereal in my mouth to punctuate my remark.

"One last thing, and please don't yell. But I think you should write Thomas a note of apology."

Just the thought turns my face bright red. "Charlotte, that sounds like something my mother would say. I mean, what if he thinks it means I want to date him? I can't handle any more attention from that direction! Although I admit I shouldn't have yelled at him."

"Just think about it."

Charlotte and I continue to talk, then wander into my room. We toe off our shoes and lie down on the bed. We stare at the swirly white ceiling while having a long conversation about boys—Robin, her crush, and George in particular.

After a while our talk goes back to the Duo.

"Charlotte, can you think of any way we could get rid of Matthew and Luke? You know, get them expelled? I think my life would be perfect then." She laughs at my idea.

"Lola, I can understand the thought, but you can't be serious. You could get in a boatload of trouble. Although on second thought, if you talked to your parents about them—"

I cut her off. There's no way I can talk to my parents without them making me explain in excruciating detail the reasons I need help. It's too embarrassing to imagine.

Before we know it, we hear the muffled jingling of keys accompanied by a clicking noise and realize my mom is walking in the front door.

Charlotte decides that's her cue to leave.

"Hi, Mrs. Potter. Bye, Mrs. Potter," she addresses my mother as she breezes out the door.

"Bye, Charlotte. Did you have a good day?" Mom calls out after her retreating back.

"Yep! Bye, Lola. See you tomorrow!" she yells over her shoulder as she continues up the sidewalk.

I give my mom a hug and ask about her class. She fills me in as she prepares dinner, but when she starts using words like *escrow*, she quickly loses my attention.

I fleetingly wonder if she remembered to pray for me yesterday. She forgot to ask me about my day, probably for the best. I'm sick of reliving it at this point, and I'll have to talk about it again with Earley later tonight.

"Is Earley coming for dinner, Lola?"

"I don't think so, Mom, but he'll be over later," I reply as I head toward my room and some privacy.

I have a huge need to lie on my bed and do nothing. I stare at the ceiling some more, then turn my eyes to the white, gauzy cotton curtains over my windows. They hardly block the light.

My eyes ease closed.

I end up taking a nap, one of my favorite things to do.

CHAPTER 6

I almost always help my mom in the kitchen after dinner. Before Elizabeth went off to college, she and I would share the cleanup. One of us would clear the table, and one of us would rinse the dishes and put them in the dishwasher. Since Elizabeth left home, Mom has taken up the slack.

"Mom, why did you offer to babysit Earley when he and Grace moved in? You know, when we were little."

"Well, I felt like Grace had a lot on her plate, being a single mom. And Earley was no problem. You and Elizabeth probably took care of him more than I did, and it kept all three of you entertained."

"Tell me some stories, please."

"Hmmm. Let me think," she responds while putting a finger up to her mouth before realizing it's covered with soapsuds from a few things that need hand washing.

"Bleh, pfft, pfft, pfft." She wipes off the soap with a dishtowel before continuing. "All three of you ran back and forth between the two houses as if you owned both places whenever Grace was home. I knew if you weren't around here, then you were at their house, so I never had to worry. And I would make the three of you take naps every day despite the fact you didn't need them—I needed one.

I found out one day when I awakened to odd slapping noises that Elizabeth had . . ."

I remember this, but it still brings a smile to my face to hear her tell it. Just as she says, she would make us lie down for a nap. So Earley and I, as the younger and smaller of us all, would share a twin bed while Elizabeth slept in her own. Sometimes we were so exhausted we did fall asleep. Other times we played quiet games across the cavernous no-man's land between the two beds, games that Elizabeth devised, where we pretended our fingers were spiders that crawled up our opponents' arms as they tried to slap us away. We knew we were not going to be in trouble as long as we stayed fairly quiet and on the beds.

While playing with Earley, we discovered that Barbie likes G.I. Joe better than Ken, that Elizabeth and I had a hidden talent for designing track for Matchbox cars, and that it was super funny to dress up little brothers in our clothes. We were happy and comfortable together. It felt like we had gained a little brother as well as a second mother. And Elizabeth and I had always wanted a little brother.

It was perfect.

I wish it still was.

After the dishes are finished, Mom and my dad turn on the television. *Fantasy Island* and *Love Boat* are on tonight.

Teresa's dad doesn't let her watch *Love Boat*. He thinks it's too risqué, but my dad (despite serving as a deacon for Teresa's dad, Pastor Dan) doesn't seem to have the same scruples. Maybe they don't discuss prime-time television at the deacons' meetings.

In the meantime and despite my earlier ability to nap, I'm getting more and more nervous; I can't seem to sit still. If Mom were to notice, she would tell me I have ants in the pants. Lucky for me, both parents seem blissfully unaware while they're engrossed in the TV.

The doorbell rings, and I freeze. Instead of being excited as usual to welcome Earley to our house, his home away from home, I feel like I'm walking toward my own execution.

I stand to go to the door, and my mom looks up at me in inquiry.

"I'll get it. It's Earley," I tell her as I reluctantly move toward the entryway.

Much to my surprise, she follows me.

Now at our tiny foyer, I pause, take a deep breath, turn the lock, and twist the knob.

"Hi, Earley," I mutter in a monotone as I pull the opening wider to allow him entrance.

Mom makes up for my deficit by greeting him with her customary enthusiasm as he opens the screen door and walks in.

"Hi, Lola. Hey, Eleanor. What's up?" he responds.

"Nothing much. Dave and I are watching TV. Lola, what are you two up to tonight?" This gives me pause for thought. Mom never concerns herself with such questions when I'm with Earley. Why now?

"Huh. Um, we'll be talking in my room for a while. You know. The usual stuff," I mumble in an awkward manner.

"Leave the door open while you're both in there, and stay off the bed," she commands in a serious voice.

"Why? I know my room's a little messy, but it's just *Earley,*" I complain. My eyes have been downcast as befits my mood, but silence greets my protest, so I chance a look at Mom and Earley to find they're staring at each other in some sort of intense silent communication.

Mom cocks an eyebrow at him, and they suddenly burst into laughter. Hers is full and throaty which means she finds my comment quite funny. Earley's is part giggle, part snicker, meaning he finds something funny, but he's holding back for some reason. And he looks self-conscious.

What's so embarrassing?

"What?" My confusion is bordering on frustration.

"Earley, would you like to explain to Lola why we're laughing or should I?" Mom asks.

Suddenly, the lines form an image. "Mom, if you're implying what I think you're implying, then Grace beat you to it about four years ago."

"Oh." Now it's her turn to blush. "I still want you to leave the door open."

Really? She surely doesn't think we're getting up to anything one flimsy wall from the den.

I huff. I've had it with both of them, so I grab Earley by the hand and yank him out the front door instead of down the hall toward my room. As we descend the front steps, the screen door slams shut behind us. I think I hear Mom clear her throat in the background.

Good grief!

Letting go of his hand and assuming he will follow, I continue my stalk toward the large magnolia tree that sits close to the front of our yard. There's a white-painted wrought-iron set with a bench, two chairs, and a small table. It's not the most comfortable, but it should work for our purposes.

Earley takes the bench, so I choose the chair in closer proximity to the side he's chosen. Close enough that I'm hoping no neighbors can hear us if they happen to walk outside or have a window cracked open.

I give Earley my most intense stare so he knows I mean business. He looks a little afraid. If I had time to think about it, this would amuse me, but we have more important stuff to discuss.

"Okay, Earley. What was all that about at lunch today?" I demand.

Earley is looking at his fingers, then toward the tree, and then at the house over my right shoulder. This is strange. He usually doesn't have problems with eye contact. I snap my fingers in his face, and he flinches.

"Hellllooooo. I'm right here. Talk!"

"Sorry, I'm not sure how to begin. I'm trying to gather my thoughts."

He takes a deep breath and gifts me with the power of his extraordinary blue gaze. (I'm pathetic. I can't help but let a little sigh escape.)

"Okay, okay, I know you heard me say those things about being self-absorbed, lack of substance, and easily distracted." I feel an internal cringe at each reminder. "Listen," he pauses, then rambles on, "Lola, I won't apologize for saying those things, although the comment about the lack of substance was way too severe, so I will apologize for *that*. I *will* apologize for saying those things to you in public, for embarrassing you, especially when you already had a bit of a bad day yesterday."

"A *bit?*" I cry out. This apology is sounding insufficient to say the least. Righteous indignation begins to simmer within my body.

"Don't . . . please don't get mad. Let me finish. Let me tell you about the many good things I see in you. You have a great sense of humor and an ability to form bonds with all sorts of people. Many people don't know this because you can be shy, but you're not a snob. I like your lack of pretention. You're intelligent—not that you always use it—you're musically inclined, you're creative, and you're loyal to your friends. But Lola, what you said to Thomas was mean, and I had to say something. And before you say it, I know none of us are perfect. Besides, can you imagine what you could say about me if you gave it a little thought?" He gives a weak chuckle.

I'm not placated.

He's still insulting me. And he doesn't understand how deeply he hurt me.

"That's just it, Earley. I don't think I would've had *anything* bad to say about you until today. Now I'm wondering about your sensitivity. And your discernment." I sniff in reproof.

This has been a couple of cruddy days.

All of a sudden, my mom is at the front door with a look of mild concern. "I was just walking by the door, and I noticed that it's sounding a bit tense out here. Everything okay?"

We must be talking too loudly. We nod, and despite our unhappy faces, she turns back to the interior of the house.

I resume with a hissed whisper. *"Why?* Why would you embarrass me in front of our friends? I consider you one of the best people I know. How can you think I'm self-absorbed and insensitive? I've never hurt you! Not only that, but Thomas was way out of line. For you to think these things of me . . ."

"Whoa, wait. I need you to listen. This is difficult for me to talk about. Okay, for the past month . . . or two . . . or more, I've been annoyed by all the little brother talk. I mean, look at me! I'm *not* Peter Pan! I'm at least six inches taller than you, but all I get is little brother this and little brother that and jokes about me growing up. I'm already grown up. I doubt I'll get much taller than this. And another thing you need to realize is I'm not your brother, little or otherwise, or in any sense of the word . . . in no way, shape, or form. Why do you think my mother and now your mother requested that we leave the door open and not sit on the bed? *Open. Your. Eyes!"*

His tone is pleading. He stops to take a deep breath before continuing, "So I think this frustration has been building, and that's why I lost it and yelled at you. I'm sorry. I don't have a good excuse, but I'm trying to help you understand."

I'm incredibly stunned by his speech. I mean, maybe he has a valid point. I just never . . . He's Earley.

"I think I get it," I murmur. I take a deep breath and realize I'm calming down. I guess I have no more energy left to expend. I must be exhausted from all the emotional ups and downs of the last few days.

I swallow. "I didn't mean to insult you with the brother stuff. You have to realize that if I had a brother, I would want him to be just like you, little or otherwise, in any sense of the word, in any way, shape, or form. Only I still can't believe you think of me the way you do. And you know what? I'm not sure I can apologize to Thomas. I don't think I'm brave enough. You have to understand how much he embarrassed me."

He sighs as only the resigned can.

"Come over here," he whispers. I smoothly switch to the bench, then I inch toward him and curl up beneath his arm. One of the nice things about Earley getting taller is that he's the perfect size to snuggle with me.

His long arms encircle me tightly, and I breathe a sigh of relief.

He even smells good. I guess he showered after practice.

"Don't be so hard on yourself," he mutters into my hair.

"It would help if you wouldn't be so critical of me, but I forgive you for saying those things today."

"You've had a few hard days, haven't you, Lowly?"

"The worst, but I'm feeling a little better now. Or maybe I'm just numb."

This makes him chuckle.

"I'm feeling better. I'm glad you're quick to forgive. We can write that one down on the positive side of your list of traits."

"Well, wait a minute. Even though you're forgiven, there is something you can do to make it up to me."

"Uh-oh. What's that?" I can tell he's grimacing even without moving to see his face.

"Recite a list of ten positive things about me at our lunch table tomorrow in front of all our friends."

"Hmm. Well, a guy's gotta do what a guy's gotta do," he declares with a theatrical shrug.

I pull back and give him a stern look, then scoot away from him. He gives me the okay sign as a blinding smile graces his lips.

Since he's a guy, I won't tell him it's sunshine.

"I'm not serious about the request," I say, "but please promise me that you'll tell me next time I exasperate you to the point of explosion. Privacy preferred, please."

He nods his head in a definitive manner.

A little while later, as we've somehow found room to spread out on the grass against a little hill at the side of the yard, tips of our fingers touching, we watch the sun set.

We're content.

I want to ask him about Pumpkin, but I'm afraid to break the serene moment. I stifle a secret, mischievous smile as I contemplate the future ammunition loaded in the gun that is my brain.

Maybe my mom did pray for me today.

I think I'll pray now.

Thank you, God, for Earley, I launch for his ears alone.

Finally, I can't help myself. I have to say it.

"I love you, Earley."

"Sure," he replies.

His flippant response squishes my content feelings like a bug beneath his size eleven shoe. I sit up and turn to face him, and he raises his face to me in inquiry.

"What's wrong?"

"Say it back."

"Why do I need to say it?"

"Just because . . . it's . . . it's . . . appropriate!"

"Appropriate?" There's a world of derision woven into his tone.

I give him a light punch to the arm.

"Ouch!" Earley yelps.

That seems an overreaction, but maybe I'm stronger than I realize.

"Lola, I've told you not to hit him," Mom admonishes in her sternest tone of voice. We look toward the house to see her bringing us some welcome lemonade on a tray. I guess she was just "passing" by the front door again.

CHAPTER 7

It's Friday night, and the football game is over. We played Kimball at Sprague Stadium and lost, but the score was closer than usual. The loss doesn't matter, anyway, because we continue to cheer despite our many defeats.

By the way, we consider the Kimball Knights our biggest rival. I'm pretty positive they don't reciprocate the regard; we always lose when we play them—in any sport. I have a suspicion we're pretty far beneath their notice.

Charlotte and I are weariness personified as we walk (or in my case, limp) away from the stadium into the parking lot, where we spot Teresa and Earley waiting near Charlotte's car.

Once the door is unlocked, the two of them hop in the back, causing me to feel relief as Charlotte and I tumble into the front.

I didn't want to squeeze back there in my uniform.

And speaking of my uniform, I need to make sure the purple and white satin doesn't get snagged on the car door. It's got this silly, stiff petticoat beneath the skirt that makes it stick out and get in the way at the worst times. If I'm not careful, I'll shut the darn thing in the door, and it'll have a permanent crease or grease stain.

After much maneuvering, I contain the fluffy monster and slam the door. I then proceed to wrench off my Bisonette boots and replace them with white Keds and a sigh. The Boots from

Hades were hurting so badly as we danced to "The Theme from Dallas" at halftime that I was crying, albeit discreetly, on the sidelines after our performance.

If I wouldn't get in trouble, I would chuck the awful boots out the window at Kimball, which adjoins the stadium, or at an unsuspecting Kimball fan.

Sometimes I'm not a very nice girl.

As the gravel parking lot rolls under the tires of the Bug, I roll down my window and throw out a shout of "*Sunset's number one!*" from a complete sense of obstinacy as we're leaving the Sprague parking lot. Take that, Kimball! We know you think we're not as good as you. Well, guess what? Kimball is as much on the wrong side of the tracks as Sunset, or maybe I should say on the wrong side of downtown.

It's a little bit stuffy, so I leave the window rolled down as we head north on Hampton Road. The wind blows over my face, calming my frustration over my painful feet, as the street goes up and down and up and down. It gets a little hilly around a few parts of Oak Cliff, and this is one of them. We pass myriads of trees, their leaves making blacker marks against a softer black sky as we breeze by; and the road crosses over several small, cliff-like ravines with creeks running through them, hence the name of this section of the city.

Soon we pass Kiest Park, where bright lights glow over one of the many baseball diamonds. No one seems to be playing. We then approach our destination, Pizza Inn.

The restaurant sits at the ugly intersection of Hampton and Illinois. Jack in the Box and El Fenix are nearby. They all nestle in and around a couple of hideous shopping centers, their old, metal-sided, brick-enhanced exteriors and neon signs dirtied with the black of car exhaust.

The beige, boxy public library branch is less than a block away.

Charlotte parks the car, and we climb out. I forgot to remove my white cowboy hat, so I take it off and toss it like a Frisbee back into the car after Earley unfolds himself from the back seat. I then proceed to shimmy out of my petticoat. It's stiff and scratchy; it needs to go.

"Lola! What are you *doing*?" I hear Teresa semishout as if offended.

"What does it look like I'm doing?" I sass and fling my discarded petticoat into the little red Bug. (It lands on the Boots from Hades.) I slam the door again for good measure.

"It looked like you were undressing in the parking lot. That's what it looked like," she huffs.

"I'm sorry. I guess I should've gone to the ladies room, but then I'd just have to walk back out to the car. That stupid petticoat is scratchy and uncomfortable. All I could think about was getting it off me." Teresa doesn't look convinced, but I feel my reply is entirely sensible.

"Give her a break, Teresa. It's not like she was removing a shirt or her skirt," Earley chimes in.

I give him a little smile and hope Teresa doesn't see it.

Actually, it's not like Teresa to correct me. She knows I'm impulsive and that I don't always think through my decisions. She usually suffers it in silence. Maybe it did look more unladylike than usual.

Of course, the root problem may be I'm not much of a lady. I look like one on the outside, but my actions often belie the outward appearance.

I walk over to her and give her a hug. "Is everything okay, Teresa?"

Her body stiffens up, and she begins to pull away from me. I sometimes forget she isn't as affectionate as Charlotte, Earley, or me; but she usually tolerates my hugs better than this.

"I'm fine, Lola. Well, I don't know. I may be a little tired and hungry."

"Okay." My sassiness has now diminished to sheepishness as we walk toward Pizza Inn.

I look over at Charlotte, who shrugs, so I turn my attention to where it should be in the first place—my path. The scrapes from my early Monday fall are hardly discernible, and I don't really feel the cut anymore, but I don't want to risk any more injury, however slight.

The usual forty-five-minute line is beginning to form outside our after-game hangout. Jack and Pumpkin are already here. The band and cheerleaders managed to arrive before the drill team and football players.

Annie and her boyfriend, Jeff, are just pulling up; they'll be in line with us. Jack is standing with some of his band friends and David, who attends the University of North Texas.

What's up with this? Pumpkin wanders back in the line to Jack, which I find curious. Most of the other cheerleaders are in front of her.

John, a church friend who attends UT Dallas, strolls up and begins talking to Teresa and Earley as a few football players begin to drive into the parking lot.

The line gets longer and longer.

Finally, George and Michelle pull up.

I lean against the wall and look at Charlotte.

"Did your boots hurt?" I query.

"No, not like yours, but my mom bought me the more expensive ones. They're pretty comfortable."

"My feet were killing me at halftime. Why did my mom not buy the leather ones?" I whine. We chatter of nothing as we wait, but we're capable of performing more than one job at a time, so Charlotte and I continue to people-watch as we talk.

John walks over, and I give him a hug. He's such a nice guy, and it's good to see him outside of church. In fact, he was a cheerleader and one of the few friendly seniors when I was a freshman.

John, Charlotte, and I continue to shoot the breeze; then Lauri drifts back toward us from where she's been hanging out with her band friends.

"Hey, Lauri. How're you feeling?" John asks. They begin a conversation, and I take the opportunity to tune out and drift into my own thoughts.

As my mind wanders, I think of George and look around for him. I soon find him and his sweetie with the other cheerleaders. They've cut, but George and Michelle don't look very happy about their prize place in line.

George catches my eye and gives me a wink, making me beam and give a saucy wink in response. My gaze flicks to Michelle as I realize what I've done. Oh, good grief! She noticed; the glare she's giving me makes me want to flee for my life. But I quell that coward's response. I'm made of sterner stuff, and I've had it with her.

She can take it out on George if she doesn't like girls responding in kind when he's friendly.

I'm pretty positive that to an outsider, the quick alteration in my expression from happy to cowed to resolute would seem funny. George must notice, because when I look back at him he rolls his eyes and grimaces.

I huff and decide I better look elsewhere.

So as Charlotte continues to talk to John and Lauri, I scoot back to Earley and Teresa. I put my arm around Earley's waist while putting the rest of my aggravated thoughts toward Michelle aside. He reciprocates, and I lean into his side. I'm tired, it's late, and I need something to eat. I'm paying for not snacking much before the game.

"Are you hungry?" he asks. I nod; he smiles down at me and squeezes me a little tighter. I smile back. He's so perfect.

"Lola, why were you flirting with George? You know he's dating Michelle," Teresa accuses out of the blue, catching me by surprise. I look over at her and notice that not only is her tone full of reproof, but her mouth is pursed up like an unhappy, old maid, like my act was so shocking that I've somehow purchased a one-way ticket to hell. How did she even see me? Earley reacts by squeezing me tighter and tighter to him as if to protect me.

"Wha? What do you mean? George gave me an innocent wink. How could anyone not return it? Hold on a minute. What's *really* wrong?" My concern and confusion grow as I try to wriggle out of Earley's too-firm grasp.

But just as I escape and reach for her, Teresa places her hand over her mouth and mumbles out some kind of apology while backing away; then races off to stand with her friends from the yearbook staff. I stand with my hand empty and outstretched toward her retreating body, longing to bring her back.

"What just happened?" I whisper. I'm stunned, and when I turn to look at Earley, he seems dazed too.

He doesn't answer me. Then I'm the one giving the hug, but I'm not sure why.

CHAPTER 8

Pumpkin strolls back to us in line, so I decide to move a little further from Earley and try to pretend that the weirdness with Teresa just now didn't occur.

It's difficult, but I put on what little game face I possess and get ready to be distracted.

"Hey, Pumpkin. The cheerleaders looked great at the game," I offer in sincerity.

Pumpkin must be a good captain, because the cheerleaders did their job well tonight. They clapped, jumped, and back-flipped as one. Maybe her abundance of sweetness and light charms those other piranhas into submission.

She replies not with words but with her angelic smile; then reciprocates the sentiment for the drill team and starts a conversation about Mr. Graham with Earley and me. Earley will have him for trig next year and has heard a ton about the teacher's eccentricities, so he pays close attention while asking interesting, funny, and intelligent questions.

He seems to have shaken off his daze over Teresa's actions. I'm not sure I have, however, and I find my thoughts drifting inward again.

I think about George and Michelle . . . George's wink . . . Teresa's accusation . . . Lauri's leukemia . . . my horrible Boots from Hades . . . Michelle's self-destructive jealousy . . . the comfort Earley and Charlotte give me . . . Annie and Jeff whispering and kissing close behind us . . . old church friends . . . the greasy bricks on the outside of Pizza Inn . . . and George's wink.

Did I mention George's wink?

Yes, all of this is going through my head as we're getting closer and closer to the door of the restaurant. Concurrently, the smell of pepperoni and cheese is getting stronger, the voices of the inside patrons are getting louder, and the jukebox is blaring "Hot-Blooded."

By the time we finally get in the door, we have to separate into two groups, and I need to pay a visit to the ladies' room. Teresa rejoins us, acting as if nothing happened; so she, Charlotte, Lauri, and I pile into a booth while Earley, John, Pumpkin, Jack, David, Jeff, and Annie perch around a bigger table where they pull up a few extra chairs.

Our two tables are close together, which works well in case we want to harass our off-table friends for no good reason, flick ice at them or whatever.

Our booth proceeds to negotiate over what kind of pizza to get, and we compromise by ordering a large Canadian bacon once our harried waitress trips by to take our order. I finally go to find the restroom, which is down a dark, dingy, cramped hallway at the back of the restaurant along with two pay phones—one broken, one not.

I emerge to find I'm not alone. Michelle and another of her friends from the cheerleading squad are leaning against the torn wallpaper lining the hallway, effectively blocking my way back to the tables.

"Excuse me." I decide to ignore them, put on a determined face, and push my way through their too-close bodies; but about four feet away Michelle puts out her hand and shakes her head no. She never even takes her eyes off the ceiling, as if she's the queen of England and too good to even look at my pitiful self.

"Yes. What is it?" I demand because I'm forced to stop. This is getting ridiculous. This hallway is too tight for the three of us and doesn't smell so great to top it off. They're not keeping me here for long, I can tell you that.

"Stay. Away. From. George," Michelle's friend, Kim, emphasizes. Kim seems to have no problem with the ugliest kind of eye contact, and she punches her right fist into her left palm as she says each word. The only problem is that Kim is about five foot of nothing but skin, bones, and blonde curls. I'm sure she still wears her first Sear's training bra. She looks like an emaciated cherub. I can't take this seriously. If it was Michelle, who is much taller and more muscular, punching her palm—and if Michelle only had the guts to look my way—I might give in to a little more fear.

"Are you serious? Listen, little Miss Trying-To-Be-Intimidating, you don't give me orders. Do you. Understand. That?" I start laughing, fold my arms, and get ready to see what their next, sad move will be.

"I'm gonna kick your butt, Lola," Kim promises as she pushes off the dirty wall to start my way.

"Oh no, you're not, you cute little faker. You stop right there, before I kick *your* skinny bottom all the way back to Sprague Stadium. And as for you, Michelle, take my advice. Control the jealousy, or you're going to lose George faster than *you* can wink.

Besides, if you don't like George being friendly with other girls, then you can take it up with him."

To add to the hilarity, Kim clenches her fists, arms straight down her sides, and lets out an ineffectual squeal of anger.

You've got to be kidding me. Oh man, I'm working hard to suppress my laughter.

"Good advice. And don't let them forget that you're friends with me, Lola," Pumpkin pipes in over Kim's shoulder. I'm not sure when she appeared. "I can make sure they don't cheer at the next few or several games if they try any more stunts like this."

Pumpkin's unexpected arrival and the impact of her words on their faces right before I roughly push through their fragile barrier of hate will provide me internal entertainment for quite a while.

Pumpkin does a talented hair fling as she pivots to return to the table; then she cuts her eyes over her shoulder to make sure I'm following her. I give her a nod of thanks in return.

We eat and play a little Pac Man. John keeps giving us quarters when we run out. Soon we're done, but Charlotte is extremely tired, so Earley suggests we ask John for a ride home. Charlotte lives not far from Pizza Inn; Earley says it wouldn't be fair to ask her to drive us, so I retrieve my discarded drill team wardrobe from her car.

"Good night, Charlotte," I call out.

"Be careful!" Teresa adds with liberal emphasis on the careful.

"Bye, everyone! Girls, I'll see y'all tomorrow night at six," Charlotte responds. We're all invited to her house for a slumber party.

Earley, Teresa, Lauri, and I squeeze into John's tiny Gremlin and head toward home.

"Did you know that yawning is contagious?" Teresa shares around one of her own yawns. The others discuss this controversial fact as John starts up his car and we roll out of the lot.

I fall asleep leaning against Earley's shoulder.

CHAPTER 9

"Come in!" Charlotte's mom yells through the door when Teresa and I knock at their tidy yellow house the next evening.

"Hi, Mrs. Gardner," we respond as we shuffle in, clutching our pillows and lazily dragging our sleeping bags behind us.

Charlotte emerges from the back of the house almost at once and beckons us to her room. Lauri and Annie are already there.

"What's up?" Teresa gets straight to the point in the sure knowledge something *will* be up as she places her overnight stuff in a corner and perches on Charlotte's bed. I follow her lead with my bags then join Lauri on the rug, sitting cross-legged beside her.

"Not much," Lauri responds. "We're trying to decide what we're gonna do."

"I say call up some boys!" Annie, ever boisterous, suggests as she commences to bounce on the bed, jouncing Teresa to the point she's almost knocked to the floor. Teresa lets out a small squeak.

"Sorry, Teresa." Annie's face is now pink-tinged with chagrin, but Teresa gives her a small smile of forgiveness in return and a pat on the arm.

"*What* boys?" Lauri's skeptical.

"Oh . . . well, Jeff, of course, and Earley, and *George?*" Annie trails off while giving me a speculative look I could do without.

Teresa, the one with good sense, quickly nips that idea in the bud.

"How about we play Truth or Dare, or How's Yours?" Annie suggests.

We all agree not to play Truth or Dare (I hope we're smarter than that) and settle on the latter game.

"How's yours?" Lauri asks us.

Ever prompt, Teresa answers with *focused,* Charlotte with *blue,* Annie with *bright and shiny,* and me with *starry.* Lauri quickly guesses eyes, the correct answer, and we continue to play.

Several hours later, with our tummies stuffed with cheeseburgers (yummy), French fries (yummier), and chocolate brownies (yummiest!); a few prank phone calls finished; and loads of gossip behind us, including my story about Michelle and Kim, we settle back to watch *Saturday Night Live.* This week, Chevy Chase reprises his role of Land Shark, and Joe Piscopo declares his love for Rose Kennedy.

Incidentally, my parents would prefer I not watch *Saturday Night Live.* I guess that's where they draw the line. I'm not sure how Charlotte's parents feel about it, but they've already gone to bed.

We eventually drift back into Charlotte's room and sink into our sleeping bags, softly talking and giggling all the while.

The later it gets, the funnier we think we are.

Then as I'm about to drift off, I hear Annie speak once more.

"Lola, I'm not surprised Michelle did that to you last night. Did anyone else notice her and George at Pizza Inn? They didn't seem happy at all. I don't think they'll last much longer. In fact, I was talking on the phone with . . ."

In my grogginess her voice is becoming part of the background, but her words cause me to remember Michelle's threat and, of course, George's wink.

The wink being a much better mental image with which to fall asleep, I smile and snuggle into the warmth and comfort of my dreams, surrounded by my friends.

Over the next few weeks of school, we discover Annie may be a prophetess, because George looks more and more unsure, contrasted with harried, and maybe even a bit angry by turns.

Or maybe Annie's just observant.

Meanwhile, Michelle exhibits continued and escalating irritability—and not just with me. Even more telling, when she's not sending evil glares, she seems sad. Her cute nose is often red, and she constantly clutches a Kleenex.

It seems as if George is no longer unruffled, and Michelle's on shaky ground. Maybe I shouldn't, but I can't help feeling sorry for her. In addition to the red nose and tissues, her beautiful hair needs a good wash, and her clothes are wrinkled and no longer match. For someone who takes immense pride in her appearance, this is telling.

She's falling apart.

In fact, within a few days of our slumber party, George sees me in the hall and stops to talk while he's holding Michelle's hand. Unlike the past, Michelle makes no effort to hide her dislike of me in front of him. Instead, she yanks her hand out of George's, gives a funny fuming noise, and stalks off with a malicious look in my direction.

Suspicious sniffles follow her as she strides away.

"Hey, George. How's it going?" I ask. I'm unsure what else to say.

"Um, I'm—I'm fine," he stutters out, shaking his head. He's staring after Michelle as she turns a corner and disappears from sight.

"Okay. See you around." I begin to move off. I don't think there's anything else to say.

"Yeah, see ya," he responds.

But my conscience prickles as I begin to leave, so I think better of it and turn back. Much to my surprise, he's not moved an inch; he looks a little lost.

"Hey, George. Wait. Is everything okay?"

As I watch, he seems to pull himself out of it. He nods decisively, looking a little more confident and like his old self. Then he gives me a small smile of reassurance.

Matthew's unwelcome and unexpected voice is the worst possible interruption.

"At least wait until Michelle is out of the picture to move in on George. Lola's a slut, George; you should watch out." My face heats in acute embarrassment, but my feelings pale in comparison to the sudden anger George displays.

I take an instinctive skip back as he turns and grabs Matthew by the beer T-shirt, yanking him closer to his body. "Repeat that. I don't think I heard you correctly," George growls in a deep, scary voice. "Or did I hear you say something about Lola that you'll be sorry you ever thought, much less uttered?"

I'm in shock. Not only that, I'm getting a liberal dose of unease. As tall as Matthew grew over the summer, George still has an inch or so on him and is much more muscular.

I don't want to get caught in any crossfire.

And I have to say, Matthew seems pretty anxious to get away from any fallout caused by his words too.

"I didn't say anything, George. Please don't tell Coach." He's almost begging.

George releases him with a snort of disgust, and Matthew staggers back a few feet. "I'm not telling Coach. I'll take care of you myself. Got it?"

As if it's my fault he can't keep his vile mouth shut, Matthew manages to get in a glare at me as he scurries down the hall with his forked tail between his legs. I don't think George sees the implied threat, because he's turned back in my direction.

I start breathing again.

"I'm sorry, George."

"Why are you apologizing? That wasn't your fault." He's gruff.

I don't have a good answer, so I shrug my shoulders.

"Listen, Lola, let me know if he gives you any more trouble." He looks worried and preoccupied again, and I feel as if I've caused it.

"I'll be fine. Remember, I'm a bobcat, right?"

"That's right. You can take care of yourself." He looks off into the distance, gives a barely audible breath, and strides off seconds before the tardy bell rings, eerily resembling the bobcat I just compared myself too.

But my assurance was hollow.

That encounter didn't leave me feeling fine in any way, shape, or form.

Ongoing, soap-operaesque scenes starring George and Michelle continue to unfold over the next few weeks.

They argue in the parking lot after school.

They sit together at lunch but don't look at each other or speak.

They stop holding hands.

A breach is looking imminent, but as much as I dislike Michelle, I can't be happy about it. They're both miserable and suffering. Even though Earley thinks I'm shallow, I can be empathetic. Seeing anyone feel pain causes me to at least feel a faint echo of sadness as well, even if she's Michelle.

And since George is involved, I'm feeling much more than a faint echo.

Then Michelle doesn't show up for school one Monday.

Before your No. 2 pencil can drop from your surprised fingers and hit the floor, the word has spread: George and Michelle have split.

George, consequently, is sitting at our lunch table when I walk in the cafeteria a little after noon.

He has a faint smile on his face when lunch is over. After all, Jack and Earley are pretty funny.

I smile too.

Once I see he has back a semblance of his old smirk, I know that, eventually, everything will be all right.

CHAPTER 10

We were twelve and felt too grown-up for children's choir.

Teresa straightens in a flash; then with more deliberation, she wipes her mouth with the back of a shaky hand to remove the evidence of some cookies she brought from home for us to share.

"I think I hear something," she whispers with a look of panic and a warning touch to my arm. My scalp begins to prickle in response.

It's Sunday afternoon and our parents have dropped us off for children's choir, but we never quite made it.

It would be really bad if we were caught skipping, especially for Teresa as the pastor's daughter. On second thought, I guess it wouldn't look so good for me as the daughter of the chairman of the deacons either.

She motions for me to follow her as she navigates her way as silent as a shadow around dusty boxes and unused choir chairs in a series of alcoves and rooms we're exploring behind the sanctuary. I trip over the edge of one of the boxes but catch myself from falling. It makes a loud thump, and Teresa turns to give me a bug-eyed look and a finger to the lips. I jerk my head in a nod and see her visibly relax. She swivels to continue on. She finally stops just to the side of a series of decorative metal screens that separate this area from the sanctuary. They have punched out holes we can look through to see out. I walk up behind her and lightly tap her shoulder to let her know I'm covering her back.

She tips her strawberry-blonde head just enough to put her eye up to the screen and look out, and I hear her sigh.

"There's no one there," she murmurs in relief.

"Good!" I say back, forgetting to speak softly. By the time I realize my mistake, she's sitting on the floor clutching her stomach with laughter. And you know what they say: laughter is contagious.

We're as good as caught.

Even more so after we find a dead mouse while looking through a box of old plastic flowers, because screaming and running don't go hand in hand with secrecy.

Although it's a welcome change—he is, after all, an incredibly charming guy. You know, good-looking, funny, kind, etc.— over the next several weeks the group dynamic begins to transform with the addition of George.

At lunch, his new seat of choice is right across from me and between Jack and Pumpkin; this suits me extremely well, because I have a ringside seat to his fineness.

But I feel compelled to confess, at first I'm too overwhelmed to add much to the lunchtime conversation. So I watch as George, Jack, and Earley talk and laugh with occasional input from one of the other girls at the table.

Jeff and Annie, meanwhile, continue to be too engrossed in each other to pay the rest of us much attention. They lean toward each other and whisper, give quick kisses, and Jeff plays with her hair. I try not to look because, well, the obvious reasons, but I'm also afraid I'll catch one of them feeding the other bites from their lunch trays. Then I'll lose all respect.

But back to George. I have to say that I *love* it when he laughs. His eyes crinkle up, and if he finds something particularly funny, he slaps the table, then looks over at me and winks.

Those winks are deadly.

Yet soon enough I get more comfortable with his presence and can't help but interject a random thought here or there in spite of myself.

I even begin to initiate conversations, albeit rather bland ones.

"What's going on this weekend other than the game?" I ask the group at large one Thursday.

"They're starting up the Bond movie again at The Astro on Saturday. I'm goin'. Anyone else want to tag along?" Jack announces.

"Sounds fun. I never got a chance to see it. What time?" I reply.

Other people nod their agreement, and even George thinks he might meet us.

Then I realize Teresa and Earley seem abnormally quiet.

"Hey, Earley, I can give you a ride if you want to go. And how about you, Teresa?" I offer because I'm pretty sure my dad will loan me his car.

But they don't respond.

So I turn to see them better. It's strange, but they seem embarrassed or maybe even guilty. Teresa looks like she's squirming a bit in her seat. Perhaps I'm misreading them, but their reactions seem out of place.

George snickers; I look over at him, and he smirks at me. I know he's trying to tell me something, but I'm not getting it.

"Teresa and I already have plans on Saturday," Earley replies after a pause that must have reached its third trimester by now. The words fall like taffy from his mouth; he lets out a quiet sigh as if he's been holding his breath.

"Is someone having a party? Maybe we can all go after the movie," I respond.

Annie perks up at the thought of a party and withdraws her attention from Jeff for the moment.

"That would be fun, but I've heard nothing about a party. I'm usually one of the first to hear," she adds with confidence and one hand to her chest.

It takes me a couple of seconds, but I process her statement and realize she's right.

So what's going on with Earley and Teresa?

Then Earley turns and looks me straight in the eyes.

I stifle a gasp at his abrupt intensity, because it's just now occurring to me what he might be about to say. A vague idea is taking shape. A few jaggedy puzzle pieces are being forced together. But it *can't* be. One of them would've let me know.

Wouldn't they?

"Lola, Teresa and I are going out on Saturday night," he says.

"We're dating," he adds after another and even bigger pause.

His statement hits me like a 747 plummeting from the sky.

I'm pretty sure my face is one big billboard advertising surprise.

But the worst is yet to come, because I look around and notice no one else is displaying the same astonishment. Nope, there's no surprise at all. Instead, they all seem to be looking at me with traces of concern, or maybe even pity in their eyes.

My face grows hot, scorching even. Then my insides begin to churn with bewilderment and mortification. Earley and *Teresa*?

Now I'm the one squirming.

"Okay?" I state. I'm sure I'm the last to know. No one else has expressed the smallest degree of shock at his revelation.

I quickly begin to comprehend, moreover, that my feelings are not only a horrifying mixture of confusion and embarrassment at being caught not in the know, but anger is mixed in there too. I know . . . I *know* I should be happy for Earley and Teresa, but instead I feel the unacceptable need to cry.

I'm not sure why.

Except this news somehow feels like a betrayal. It feels like everyone else was in on the joke, but I wasn't considered friend enough or mature enough or worthy enough to be let in on it.

I was left out.

I *am* the joke.

I glance over at Teresa; she's looking concerned and relieved, and I see her clutching Earley's hand.

She's holding it with both of her own.

She's holding it as if she'll *never* let it go.

This is too much.

"Okay. Well, have fun. I'll see you all later. I, um, just remembered I need to head to the library to look for a book before my next class." I sound resentful at the least, but I'm unable to care. Then I can't help myself: I have to say something, even though I regret it before it even passes my lips.

"And by the way, Earley and Teresa, I don't appreciate being the last person to be told of your relationship. It's obvious that I'm the only one who wasn't informed. Thank you for making me look like a fool. I guess I'm so unimportant that you couldn't take five minutes to tell me."

I hear a gasp and realize it came from Teresa. "Lola, how can you say that?"

I'm pretty sure she doesn't expect an answer to such a stupid question. I bite my lip to keep it from trembling and push my chair back, because I'm not going to let two betrayers see me cry. It makes its typical racket when I push it back in. It seems louder than usual in the silence that has fallen around us. But I don't look up to see the group's reaction to the noise, or to see their reaction to my words, or anything, because I don't want to look at *anyone* right now.

Jack calls out the time for the movie Saturday night as I'm turning to walk away. I'm unable to process his words, but I glance over my shoulder to vaguely nod in his general direction.

I feel as if I'm in some sort of strange vacuum as I carefully walk out of the cafeteria. No sound penetrates it. No nothing.

A loud clattering breaks the silence, and I realize I'm free of the doors. The banging is the noise they make when they're not closed with care. But I'm out. So I sprint down the hall searching, wondering where I might go to hide for a few minutes. I decide the library is not such a bad idea after all and turn a sharp left to bound up the stairs to the third floor.

I'm not sure why I feel so hurt, so angry, and so confused about this news. But I don't do well with change, and I don't do well with secrets being kept from me or with embarrassment, so I'll start with working through those three things and go from there.

And I hate it. I *hate* that I'm like this. I hate it when I cry, but my eyes are overflowing by the time I get to the library.

I eke out a sniffly hello for the librarian; she pretends not to notice, so I grab a handful of Kleenex from the box on her desk and continue to a table in the back by a window. It's hidden from the rest of the room by bookshelves.

Instead of sitting down, I walk to the window and lean my forehead against it, trying to shut down the tears.

The sun has heated the glass in the familiar way of late-summer Texas days. It's a hot, prickly kiss against my sweaty forehead.

It fits my mood, so I stay there, fists balled at my sides, leaning against its smudgy surface.

I start to pray, hoping God can make something out of the tangle of my thoughts.

God, why? Why would they do this to me? Help me not to feel this. Make me numb.

But I continue to be lost in inexplicable grief and resentment until subdued footfalls penetrate my erratic thoughts. Someone's walking up behind me. A hand is on my shoulder.

A sound of relief escapes my lips once I look over to discover George. Charlotte walks up behind him; she looks a little teary herself.

And I shouldn't, but I practically collapse on George, squeezing him for all I'm worth, gluing my head to his windpipe. I think I may be cutting off his supply of oxygen, and I'm sure my tears are soaking his shirt, but I'm in huge need of comfort and pretty well past concern or timidity.

"Why didn't they tell me? They *are* my friend*s*, right?" My words are disjointed. "Why do things have to *change?*" I sob, and with that statement I almost get to the crux of the matter.

It's a blessing that no one tries to answer. They're smarter than that.

"He's not hers. He's *mine,*" I grind out in an almost inaudible whisper and cringe. I hate myself a little bit for saying it and vow never to say it again.

I hope Charlotte and George didn't hear.

They might misunderstand, I tell myself.

Then I remember. And I realize George's hands are no longer soft and small.

Instead, they're large and strong, but they hold comfort still.

Over the next few weeks, things continue to evolve.

Our new lovebirds are an item. They walk together hand in hand; Earley often gives her a quick kiss at her locker.

I feel some kind of strange, sharp pain each time I witness one.

But Teresa blossoms and blooms at those kisses.

So I try not to think about the affection they exchange in private.

I try to act as if nothing has altered.

It's not working.

"Earley, are you coming over to dinner tonight? You haven't been over in forever, and my mom is missing you," I cajole on the ride home from school one afternoon.

Who am I trying to kid? So I try for pathetic.

"*I'm* missing you," I say under my breath. He hears me but doesn't address my second remark. He ignores it. He ignores me, just as he has for the past two weeks. In fact, he never acknowledged my response to his announcement that day in the cafeteria.

"I can't come over tonight. Teresa is coming to my house, and we're studying together. Tell Eleanor I'll try and make it over soon." He sounds as if he hasn't a care in the world.

He sounds so . . . *happy*.

But he no longer calls me Lowly, and I continue to feel betrayed.

Too bad I can't beat Teresa off with a stick like the hordes of other girls I was ready to defend him against at the beginning of the school year.

We stop in front of my house as usual, and as part of our new routine, Charlotte turns off the car and gets out with us. Ever since Earley and Teresa started dating, Charlotte tries to spend more time with me. Instead of leaving me alone on the sidewalk missing Earley as he turns his back on me and walks away, she stays more often than not.

She stays because, well, she's a good friend, and she's trying to fill the hole Earley has left in my life.

I'll admit I was skeptical. I thought her efforts would be fruitless, but after a few weeks, I'm glad to be proven wrong.

One such afternoon, as we're scarfing Bluebell in the kitchen, Charlotte broaches the subject of our young lovers.

"She's not good enough for him, Charlotte." My bitterness is showing.

"You don't mean that," she chides.

Yes, I do, but her words arrest my anger for the moment; Charlotte rarely corrects me. So I look at her for a minute, take a deep breath, and think about my statement.

I think about my past with Teresa. I think about the laughs and secrets we've shared and remember that she's usually one of the first to learn when I've been hurt or offended. I think about the times her mother's fed me wonderful food, taken care of me, and welcomed me to her home without warning. I think about the times Teresa and I have skipped church to pray together. And the time we snuck out of her house in the middle of the night only to get to the end of her driveway and turn our scared, thirteen-year-old bodies right back around. I think about the times we've laughed so hard we could barely breathe. Then I think about Teresa's gentleness, her steadiness, and about the times her example has steered me in the right direction.

"I don't," I concede with a little bit of shame thrown in for good measure, then add, "I'm not being fair to Teresa."

"Nope, you're not. But I will say this. I think, at present, they deserve each *other* pretty well," she says and then grins at me. I guess I'm not the only one they've been ignoring.

"You're a devil, Charlotte."

"I know."

We laugh and laugh and laugh at her joke.

Then the part of my heart that belongs to Earley begins to heal.

CHAPTER 11

As cliché as it sounds, life goes on.

Matthew and Luke continue to harass me any chance they get (e.g. "You're a *ho!*"), and I continue to remind them I'll tell George about their remarks, which continues to shut them up. Charlotte and Lauri continue to bring me back to earth. George continues to talk to me and wink. Teresa and Earley continue to cuddle way too much, from which I continue to look away. Schoolwork, choir, drill team, and church activities continue to keep me busy.

Overall, things are getting better.

Then one day at lunch, as Pumpkin hums something that sounds suspiciously like "For Your Eyes Only" under her breath, her name inadvertently gives me a brilliant idea.

"Hey! We need to go buy pumpkins. The farmers' market probably has all their pumpkins, gourds, and chrysanthemums out," I exclaim, sounding way too much like an advertisement.

Everyone laughs at my enthusiasm; then the guys let out a few groans. But for once, instead of getting defensive, I look around and give them a smile. My idea is still brilliant, even if they're all too dense to see it.

"No, no, and no," Jack denies any interest in my proposal while punctuating his negativity by shaking his head and looking dramatically off into the distance.

"I think that's a great idea," Charlotte seconds, and that's all the encouragement I need.

"Okay. Who's in?" I ask with energy, and with much less coaxing than the groans foretell, everyone wants to join us.

Just to give you a little background, Teresa, Charlotte, Earley and I have been going to the farmers' market together in the fall, with or without our families, for the last several years. We love it, despite Earley's token guy moan.

My mom loves it too, because it saves her a trip, and with my assistance, she takes what I bring home and creates wonderful decorations for our front porch. Then right before Halloween, my friends and I gather back together to carve a few of them up.

Furthermore, it's now Wednesday, September 30, meaning the first weekend of October is upon us. Everyone knows that early October is the perfect time to start the pumpkin-buying process.

"Who can drive?" I query. Our group has grown to ten people. We may have to take three cars, but George and Jack volunteer; since they can each take five (or in Jack's case six), we're good.

In short order, we decide to leave around noon on Saturday and grab some lunch while we're there. After all, the aforementioned pumpkins, flowers, and gourds aren't the only things they sell at or near the Dallas Farmers' Market.

Our planning carries on, and we agree that I'll be riding with George because we live in close proximity. Charlotte and Lauri are spending the night with me after the game, so he's offered to take them as well.

It's a shock, but Earley decides to ride with us too.

All of a sudden, George starts up his characteristic snickering.

"Earley, do you think you and Teresa can stand to ride in separate cars? Lately, you've been wrapped around each other so tightly I'm beginning to think of you as the same person."

We all begin to laugh except Teresa and Earley. They're looking a little awkward.

"Ha, ha," Earley replies in a sarcastic tone, his face sporting a distinctive blush of embarrassment.

"That's all you've got, Earley?" I tease. "I think you can do better than that. Don't let George give you a hard time. He's just a big bully, but *I* can protect you from him if you're not up to the task."

I cock my eyebrow, purse my lips, and look over at George with a challenge to find his jaw has dropped in astonishment. And actually, I myself am a little astounded at my joking.

Without warning, George lunges across the table, ruffles my hair, and (even worse) takes my Boston cream pie.

This is a problem. It's the only dessert I find halfway decent in this place.

"Cake thief! Unhand that slice, you dastardly dessert pirate," I demand.

"No way. You need to remember to respect your de facto leader. If you're not careful, I'll make you do the sophomore clap and carry my tray."

"What? I'm not a sophomore, and no way am I carrying your tray." I put on my snootiest voice. "Now if you're lucky, I might give you a kiss on the cheek to get it back."

"You tell 'em, Lola! But dessert pirates don't like kisses on the cheek—they're too tough to be cajoled like that," Jack responds as he grabs my cake away from George and hands it back.

"Hey! I'm not that tough," George pouts.

Everyone laughs at his joke but Earley.

I'm just about to take a big bite of my dessert when the bell rings.

C'est la vie, I think; then I remember George tousling my hair, and it gives me a tiny shivery feeling.

Saturday comes around, and we're all piling into George's car as planned except Earley.

I shouldn't be surprised. He's somehow found a way to hitch a ride with Jack, who is taking Teresa.

The six of them will be tightly packed into Jack's car, despite its gargantuan size, but if Earley is so enamored of Teresa that he can't stand to be away from her for the fifteen-minute drive down to the market, then they can all enjoy being sardines together. Furthermore, I think they have become the same person, just as George said. In fact, I may start calling them Turdley (at least in my head).

In the meantime, we'll be comfortable riding in George's navy blue Oldsmobile Cutlass. We're cozy, not crammed, listening to his eight-track and belting out "Super Freak" for all the world to hear. The windows are rolled down, of course.

We arrive with what we think is a flourish and park in the Harwood lot; then we exit our cushy transportation and look around for Jack's car.

We soon spy a large, blue land yacht (also known as Jack's 1970 Lincoln Continental) pull into the lot and know the rest of our group has arrived.

They spill out of Jack's car, and despite my earlier internal disparagement, none of them look as if they've been uncomfortable during their trip. Drat. Annie leaps out and commences jumping around in happiness. Jeff follows, looks on, and laughs with indulgence. Jack is talking to Pumpkin as she smiles her serene smile and exits the car with grace. Lastly, Earley helps Teresa from the vehicle; they continue to hold hands after she emerges from the back seat.

We greet each other, and I may be imagining it, but Earley and Teresa seem to have the same slightly defiant look on their faces. They must be remembering George's comment from lunch a few days ago.

So be it.

My mind, however, quickly wanders away from Turdley, and I take note of our surroundings. The weather is glorious. It's cool and brisk. Perfect.

And if the weather is a feast for our often overheated bodies, the market itself is a banquet for our eyes. Crisp, prickly hay bales support precariously balanced pumpkins in huge orange mounds. Surrounding them are colorful bunches of Indian corn, gourds of fascinating grotesquerie, and pristine chrysanthemums in every shade in which they bloom. Deep, mysterious purple; flashy gold; wounded red; and earthy, subtle brown flowers surround us, not a satin-soft petal out of place.

It's as if my surroundings are cleansing me, helping me to shed the last vestiges of my sadness, my bitterness, for the moment. Who could be upset on day like this? I mean, we're together, and we're blessed. We may not be able or willing to articulate it, but we feel it.

Everyone is content.

We're also hungry.

We scramble across the street toward a burger place for lunch.

A reckless car honks its horn, narrowly missing us. In our youth and exuberance, we aren't disturbed enough that it might have been a close call. "Slow down!" we catcall. "Watch it!"

The driver responds with his middle finger.

"Nice," I say but soon forget the incident in my need to eat. I'm hungry, and a cheeseburger is calling my name.

We gather round the cash register and overwhelm the poor cashier with our boisterousness, but eventually, we all sit down to eat and talk—not at the same time, I hope. A few of us have atrocious manners (I'm speaking about the guys, of course.).

We finish our greasy food and toss our trash; then George makes sure we cross the street with a little more caution this time.

We head toward one of the pavilions but quickly detour because it holds more of the food-type items. With our stomachs full, we're more interested in autumn decorations than food per se, and most of the pumpkins, gourds, and mums are set up in uncovered vacant lots adjacent to the other buildings.

We wander about and get separated. George, Charlotte, and I remain together, strolling along and discussing the merits of the perfect pumpkin. Charlotte and I discover we need to educate George in the fine art of pumpkin selection.

"It shouldn't be perfect." I personify patience while running my hands along the dusty, smooth surfaces of the group of pumpkins nearest me.

"Lola's right. Character is more important than perfection, although you need to make sure there aren't too many deep bruises or any gouges," Charlotte sagely adds.

"It's also important that the pumpkins you select complement each other," I say.

"Okay, ladies, I think we should get started. How about this one?" George picks one up at random, and even though it lacks character, Charlotte and I, in unspoken agreement, decide we'll let it slide. We'll use it as a start for our decorating tableau.

"Looks good. Let's find one larger and more oval to go with it," I suggest.

We continue to walk around and buy autumn bounty, yet we soon find our purchases are getting too heavy to carry. We're almost at our weight limit when our paths cross with Jack and Pumpkin. Their arms are as loaded as ours, and they're heading to Jack's car to drop off their parti-colored orange cache. Charlotte decides to join them; George and I agree. So we all start toward the cars to load our weighty acquisitions into the trunks.

George inserts his key, twists, and the Oldsmobile's trunk opens with a nice, quiet, hydraulic whoosh. Not far away, Jack's trunk creaks and groans awake in a manner very appropriate for the season. The pumpkins tumble inside, and we try to separate them out by purchaser but quickly give up; we'll deal with the problem later.

As we're walking back to find more of our group, Charlotte spots Lauri walking by herself and decides to ask her to join us. She's in the middle of buying some flowers, so Charlotte waits, leaving George and me alone for the moment.

Jack and Pumpkin seem to have wandered off again.

"Do you have any plans for homecoming?" he starts.

Good grief. Did the sun just fade a bit? I really don't want to think about homecoming. It's in a few weeks, and I have yet to be asked to the dance. I guess I'll have to ask someone from another school.

Again.

I'm not sure how to respond, so I garble out something meaningless while looking at the ground.

"What was that?" George teases. "You're not making any sense."

"Oh, um, sorry. I was just saying that I don't have any plans yet. I mean, I'm obviously going to the game. It's required. You know, drill team."

"We-ell," he singsongs, "How about we go to the dance together?"

My eyes bug out in disbelief. I quickly raise them to his face because I can't believe he's serious.

He doesn't, however, appear to be joking.

"As friends . . . only because . . . well, I'm not sure if I want to spell it out, but the reasons have nothing to do with *you*. Believe me," he mumbles, looking a little more self-conscious the longer he talks.

I think over his words and decide to take them at face value; then I smile a slow smile and think on how to respond, not what to respond.

Parce que c'est un jour fantastique, as we say in French class.

CHAPTER 12

It's the Friday night before the homecoming dance, and the football game is going strong.

We're playing Adamson; they're one of the few teams with an even more abysmal win record than our own.

Although I have to admit we're having a pretty good year football-wise. So far, we've won about half of our games. That's pretty much unprecedented over the last two hundred years or so. (I'm just kidding. It's more like the last three decades.)

But more important than our win record, I'm feeling pride tonight as I sit in the stands, because George has given me a humongous mum to wear to the game. Even better, it wears his football jersey number on its face, causing me to gain a new appreciation for purple pipe cleaners.

I'm thinking this proves George isn't embarrassed to be going with me to the dance.

I'm walking on cloud nine, so as we perform our half-time routine, I try to dampen my enthusiasm a little. I'm so excited that I'm afraid I'll leap too high or spin too fast, and that won't do. After all, drill team is about performing as a unit. The more synchronization, the better we look.

But as is my tendency, once halftime is over and we're back in the stands and seated, my mind takes a little detour. This time it heads straight to the dress I'm wearing to the dance.

Mom and I went shopping for it last Saturday. We didn't have a lot of time (Mom is busy with classes during the week, and the shops aren't open on Sunday), so we were in for quite the marathon.

You should've seen us—we were on a mission. We flew into store after store, elbowing our way through the crowds, but we finally ended up at a designer dress outlet down in the warehouse district of West Dallas. It's not a pretty area of town, if the truth be told, but Mom said this designer sells his dresses to Neiman's and other high-end department stores. She said we're pretty lucky to get his leftovers at a discount.

The door gave a happy jingle as we entered the nondescript building. The shop itself was bare bones, but they must've decided to decorate with the merchandise to save money, because when we entered, we were greeted by dresses of every color crammed into every conceivable space. They graced the walls and were smushed onto the racks. I'm surprised they didn't hang from the ceiling as well.

Our eyes and fingers found taffeta, tulle, and silk. Some were constructed of velvet, and some chiffon. Some were white, some pink, or blue, or purple, or green, or multicolored. And the dresses were decorated with sequins and lace of every imaginable shape and hue. It was like walking into a sparkly rainbow that had exploded again and again.

And again.

We found my size, and Mom began to dig through the rack with the determination of the very seasoned shopper that she is. She found a pink one, and I found a dark green one to try on. Then like a fairy godmother with a magic wand, she conjured up a strapless navy dress with silver sequins on the bodice and a velvet skirt. I loved it, but Mom thought it might be too fancy for the homecoming dance.

We decided to try it on anyway.

I tiptoed around the pins and needles dropped willy-nilly in the cramped changing room, avoiding them despite the slight chaos and rustle of pulling all the layers over my head; then Mom zipped me up.

We fell in love.

I wake up from my reverie when the marching band begins playing "Long Train Running." The Bisonettes perform a short routine in the stands whenever the band plays this song, so I need to pay attention.

On second thought, I can do this routine in my sleep. What difference will it make if I daydream? But after we're done, I try to concentrate on the game despite the temptation to let my mind wander.

"Go, Bisons!" we yell over and over.

Later, as George is driving Teresa, Earley, and I home from Pizza Inn, I continue to think about the dance.

I can't seem to stop. I have an out-of-place smile on my face.

I hope no one notices, because it's a bit embarrassing.

The next day passes too quickly.

Soon it's time to get ready for the dance, so I push myself up from the couch where I've been watching television to take my mind off my nervousness.

After all, this is probably the most time I've spent one-on-one with George since we were in preschool.

I take the hot rollers out of my hair, begin to brush it out, and then start the process of putting on my dress.

I pull it over my head, and it swishes and slides to the floor. I'm momentarily distracted from getting ready by the dress's image in the mirror. The velvet skirt has a multitude of gathers that blossom out from my waist like an upside-down flower. Silver sequins flow like rivulets of water away from the petals up the bodice.

I still think it's beautiful . . . not a surprise.

Once ready, I twirl and twist in front of my reflection, hoping everything is perfect. I know George says he wants to go with me as friends. That's fine with me, but maybe I can begin to change his way of thinking.

Then I realize I'm kidding myself. George is not for someone like me. So I decide on a more realistic approach. I decide to look my best and behave my best, and thereby I'll not have any reason to regret the evening when all is said and done.

After all, it wasn't so long ago he was getting over his big breakup with Michelle. They'd been together for over a year, so I imagine going with someone else tonight will feel a little strange to him.

The doorbell chimes out; I stop fussing and take a deep breath.

I hear my mom answer the door, George's deeper voice in response, and then my father's even deeper tones.

I step out of my room into the hallway that leads to the den. When I arrive in the living room I'm a little wobbly on my new silvery heels, but I'm not uncoordinated and will soon get the hang of walking in them.

"Hi, George." I'm feeling a bit self-conscious, but I can tell he isn't. He looks fantastic wearing his usual confidence, a dark gray suit, and a navy tie, but I didn't expect any less. He's George, after all.

"Hi, Lola. Are you ready?"

"Wait! Dave wants to take a few pictures," Mom interjects.

Meanwhile, like a magician from a hat, George pulls out a beautiful wrist corsage from thin air and plops it down on the dining room table. I'm sure it's for me, but he doesn't say anything.

So I just stand there staring at it.

"It's for you, Lola," he says with a suppressed smile on his face as if he's trying not to laugh at my reaction.

"Oh, of course!" I respond in slight surprise at his directness. I pause and realize I'm still being awkward. "*Wow.* Thanks. It's beautiful," I continue.

I grab the box but have difficulty opening it, so he removes it from my hands and pulls the delicate, pure white flower from its confinement.

He holds it up between us; I know I'm supposed to take it, but sometimes it feels right to just stop and take everything in.

But I don't think George is of the same mind.

"Why are you staring at it? Take it," he commands.

"Okay," I murmur.

So I carefully take it from his palm where it rests and pull the strap over my hand.

There now. That's a great place for it. It's right where it belongs. If I wish, I can admire it all night from this vantage point.

But my mind is quickly drawn away by the arrival of my dad with the camera.

Click! Click!

A few seconds later we're smiling into the lens; Dad (believe it or not) is directing us to stand closer. George puts his arm around me and pulls me in.

It feels strange to be leaning into his side like this. It feels as if I don't quite belong, or maybe, it just feels new.

Different.

But I shake off the uneasy thought as we're taking the pictures, and when I look up at George, I find him genuinely grinning at the camera.

Dad continues to click away.

Before we know it, we're in the car and heading to dinner. I'm excited; George is taking me to some fancy-schmancy restaurant. The food is supposed to be over-the-top.

I order chicken with some unpronounceable French name by pointing to it on the menu; he orders prime rib.

The only downside happens before the meal, when I eat my salad with freshly ground pepper. Something about it gets caught in my throat and makes me choke in an uncouth fashion. My eyes tear up as I gulp down water from my sparkly water glass to try to rectify the situation. George starts laughing when he sees I'm okay, and once I catch my breath, I can't help but admit it's pretty funny (albeit humiliating). Anyway, my new motto is: No freshly ground pepper.

The upside of the incident is that it breaks the ice. I've now committed a major faux pas at one of the nicest restaurants in

Dallas. If George isn't running for the hills by now, then I guess things are looking good, and I can relax a bit more.

"You're so funny, Lola," he manages to get out between chuckles; then he sighs and throws himself back against the black leather banquette as if he's run an amusement marathon and is now out of breath.

"Um, thanks, I guess," I reply, but my mind is already headed toward dessert. I'm wondering what kind of sugary gems they offer at a place like this.

My thoughts are pulled back to the present by the plate of chicken something being precisely placed in front of me by a waiter with a thin little mouth and what seems to be a stick up his back. I smile at him in thanks, but he pivots on his heel and quickly stalks off to the kitchen.

My choking must have offended him.

After a meal of the best chicken something I've ever tasted and a slice of dark chocolate cake so rich that I'm surprised it didn't put me into a coma, I decide I don't care if it did offend him.

We get into the car and zoom toward the dance. It's being held at the Oak Cliff Country Club, as it is every year, and as we drive up to the building, we notice all the other students streaming toward the front entrance.

We park, look at each other, and exit the car simultaneously.

But as we walk toward the building, I regain my earlier self-consciousness.

People are staring.

This is not an uncommon occurrence when George is around.

Consequently, we enter the double glass doors to the greetings of George's many friends. Of course, he's intensely popular, being the student body president. He handles it with a lot of grace.

But I'm not comfortable with all the attention, so I go into denial mode. This means I just try to ignore it.

We hear music as we enter the club lobby, and even though the DJ is in full swing, the dance has just opened and the dance floor is empty. George and I get in line to get our pictures taken, then drift over to a table with some of his senior friends. Jack and Pumpkin are sitting there. Jack looks snazzy, but a little uncomfortable in his suit and tie. I've never seen his normally straight but windblown hair looking so orderly, and I wonder how he accomplished it.

I find it interesting that Jack and Pumpkin are here together as friends. Her ever-cautious parents with their no-dating rule relented about the dance since it's her senior year. The dating boycott has some nebulous religious reason that I've never felt comfortable asking about, but it drives the boys crazy that she's off-limits. Within their purported character, however, Mr. and Mrs. Evans (Pumpkin's parents) volunteered to chaperone as an added condition to her date.

For now, the Evanses are standing in a corner, talking to a few other adults, including a couple of teachers. Periodically, they glance with seeming benevolence over at Pumpkin. It's funny, but they don't look like the jail wardens they're supposed to be. Instead, they talk and laugh with the other adults and seem to be enjoying themselves.

In all likelihood, we'll forget their presence once the dancing commences.

I notice Charlotte and Lauri sitting at an adjoining table with their dates, Sam and Petey. Teresa and Earley sit on the opposite side of the table, engrossed in each other and oblivious to all others; Annie and Jeff sit next to them cuddling.

The girls are glittering, colorful jewels in their many-hued dresses. The boys look handsome in their suits. But other than Earley, not one boy holds a candle to George.

George and I walk over to say hello; then he pulls me back over to the table with Jack and Pumpkin. We sit down and discuss our evening's dining experiences. George decides to tease me about the pepper incident, but he lowers his voice to make sure only Jack and Pumpkin hear about it. I smile in response and publicly swear off freshly ground pepper forever.

My words make Pumpkin smile and Jack laugh.

I look around during a lull in the conversation and notice Annie is no longer content to lean against Jeff but is fidgeting in her seat. Suddenly, she jumps up to run to the dance floor, surprising him in the process. He seems happy, as usual, to stumble off in her wake. They arrive on the dance floor, joining a few other brave bodies, and he almost collides into her back when she precipitously stops. Annie immediately begins twirling and jumping and moving in all her glorious Annie ways.

Jeff tries to keep up.

We can't all be Annie, but her enthusiasm is contagious. Before you know it, the dance floor is filled with happiness.

We're spinning and color and sound. We're beat and flow and synchronization.

We personify fun.

After all, dancing is freedom.

Dancing is joy.

I stop to catch my breath and notice Teresa is momentarily without her recent appendage.

And it hits me: I really miss her.

I don't miss her as much as I do Earley, I have to admit, but when George excuses himself to get us something to drink, I decide to go over and talk to her for a few minutes.

"Hey!" I shout over the noise.

Teresa smiles a welcome but self-conscious smile and shouts back. "Are you having fun, Lola?"

"Very much!" I yell, and it's time for me to look a little awkward at my exuberant declaration. Teresa laughs at my enthusiasm, then becomes serious all at once.

She leans in to be heard. "Listen. I'm sorry Earley and I have been so . . . neglectful of our friends since we started dating."

At her words, my mood starts to take a slight downturn, and I look down at the ground, not sure how to answer. I've forgiven Teresa and Earley for their self-absorption for the most part, but it still hurts to think about the manner in which I discovered their relationship.

I take a deep breath and look up. "I don't know, Teresa. Thanks but I'd rather not talk about it right now."

"Sure. But maybe we could get together and talk soon."

"Yeah, maybe," I mouth and nod.

Teresa ignores my reluctance and compliments my corsage and dress; I reciprocate. It's a tiny bit difficult for me, but I confide to her how handsome I think Earley looks in his suit. She blushes and nods in agreement.

Like a genie from a bottle, George reappears, hands me some water, and smiles his distracting smile at me. At its heart-speeding appearance, I melt a little bit like the ice in my glass.

I'm a silly girl.

Then he grabs my hand, and we head back to the dance floor.

A few minutes after we arrive, a slow dance starts, and unabashed, he pulls me close. Being near to him still feels a bit off or maybe even risky, but I wrap my hands around his neck as we begin to sway to the music.

Crisp, clean wool is under my fingertips. I'm close enough to catch his aftershave or something.

I love it when guys smell good.

George is fantastic! Forget Earley . . . for a while.

Then I notice Michelle and Kim standing at the side of the dance floor, heads together, giving me identical dirty looks.

CHAPTER 13

It's Sunday morning, and Teresa, Lauri, and I are sitting together in church. I know we shouldn't be, but we're passing notes back and forth while trying to keep a straight face over some of Lauri's humorous observations on the human condition.

The head usher tests our resolve when he drops the offering in close proximity to us. He whispers a quiet "Oh, darn!" under his breath as he tries to stoop and pick up the plate's contents. He's not very mobile at this point in his life, so it's presenting him a bit of a problem. Earley who is sitting closest to the aisle, slips out of the pew and bends to help the elderly man pick up the stray checks, bills, and change without any prompting.

Earley's a good guy.

The thought sobers me up right away and reminds me of the meeting I've planned with Teresa this afternoon—a meeting to which I agreed despite my initial reluctance.

I'm soon diverted, however. As we stand to sing another hymn, little Joseph Caldwell, sitting in the pew in front of our group, turns toward us. His chubby little finger is in the air; much to our dismay, it's proudly sporting a *huge* booger. He tries to flick it at us. We simultaneously dive below the pew to take cover until we hear his mother, who has only now caught on, grab him and drag him out of the sanctuary to wash his hands.

The musicians carry on as if nothing untoward has occurred, but as we return to our previous positions and look back toward the pulpit, we notice Pastor Dan, Teresa's father, pinching the bridge of his nose and shaking in silence; he's trying to stifle his own mirth.

I guess he caught the action.

When he looks up, his eyes are twinkling. I think the effort to hold in his laughter is causing them to water.

Welcome to a typical Sunday morning at Calvary Baptist Church of Oak Cliff.

Once he's behind the pulpit, Pastor Dan seems ready to put the laughter behind him and talk to us about forgiving others from Matthew 6.

I'm not sure I'm ready to hear this message, but maybe it's time for me to forgive Teresa and Earley. And stop calling them Turdley in my head. I guess I need to be straightforward with Teresa and tell her I'm not giving up on Earley's friendship, even though it seems as if he doesn't care about mine anymore.

I hear the doorbell ring and know she's arrived.

"I'll get it!" I yell as I rush to the door.

I manage a smile as I let Teresa in. "Hey, I need to change into jeans; then we could walk to Minyards and get some Bluebell to take to the park. What do you think?"

"Sounds like you have it all mapped out," she kids me in her gentle voice.

She's right. I have given it some thought and don't want to talk at my house. I just shrug and motion her back to my room.

We happen to pass George's house on our way to the park, prompting Teresa to ask me for more details about our night at the dance.

"It was great, Teresa. He's pretty incredible. But I don't think he would ever want anything more from me than friendship," I respond in complete sincerity.

"Why would you think that? You're pretty great yourself."

"Thanks, but he's George. I'm not sure I can expect anything else. Frankly, it's a little out-of-character for you to encourage me to start taking flights of fancy. What's going on?"

She blushes a little. "I guess I'm thinking it's probable that you've been missing Earley. Maybe God is sending you George to help with that."

Huh. So that's why she's saying this—she wants to take my focus off Earley. I mean, she's normally sensible, and I've not once witnessed her being outright territorial, but that's close to how this appears.

Moreover, and to be frank, there's no one who can replace Earley, not even George. There's too much history to our relationship. Furthermore, Earley is Earley, and George is George. You can't just replace one with the other like they're each a pair of jeans or different flavors of ice cream. I raise my brows in skepticism, but I can't think of words to reply.

We park our bottoms on the u-shaped swings and quickly dig out the plastic spoons I scavenged from the back of our pantry along with a few wrinkly napkins.

Prying off the lids and digging into our sweet, cold Bluebell, we're careful not to break our fragile spoons.

The swings are the soft kind, made of plastic or rubber, and they cradle us a little too tightly at our age; yet, in our sugar-induced euphoria, we handle the slight discomfort well. We even manage to forget about boys for a few minutes.

We swing and eat and laugh just like old times.

Then the thought of the almost-break in our relationship recalls me to the purpose of our visit.

This is my second sobering thought of the day.

Yuck.

I try to put off the awkward part of the conversation a smidgeon longer by bringing up the little delinquent's revolting act at church this morning.

"That was disgusting!" I declare, placing plenty of necessary emphasis on the last word.

"I know, I know," Teresa replies, nodding while trying to wipe some ice cream from her chin. She's had a little mishap while we were laughing.

Unfortunately, it doesn't take her long to remember the purpose of our meeting, so she looks at me and gets to the point.

"Lola, I guess we need to talk."

I glance over at her but don't respond right away. I must look like Penelope Pitstop tied to the tracks of a massive rusty train.

"Come on. You know we do," she coaxes and then smiles at me with her sweet smile.

I look down, suddenly feeling even more ill at ease. This meeting was her idea, but I decide not to resist her prompt. So I gather my nerve and begin to blurt out the words that will convey my disjointed thoughts.

"Teresa, why was I the last to know about you and Earley?"

I realize with relief that I've done a better job at cutting to the chase than I anticipated.

It's now Teresa's turn to look at the ground and pause.

"Earley asked me not to tell you, Lola, and unfortunately, I agreed." Loaded pause, then she confesses, "He intended to tell you himself before it became public knowledge. I've asked him why he didn't do it, and he's never really answered me. I'm not sure why no one else ever mentioned it to you. Maybe they assumed you already knew."

As she speaks, her voice is laced with notes of slight exasperation; she looks uncomfortable.

"I'm sorry," she adds.

She finally looks up at me.

I guess she's sincere.

I look away. "Teresa, I was beyond embarrassed, but that was just the beginning. Earley acted (he still acts) as if I've hurt him instead of vice versa. And you do too. You both hurt me and continue to. But at least you're making an effort now. He hardly talks to me; he does everything he can to avoid me. I've tried to talk to him about it, but he's become a master of escape. Houdini has nothing on him."

I pause to let out an ironic chuckle.

"He was my best friend. I *miss* him."

My voice escalates, reflecting my rising frustration. "I understand that, for whatever reason, he feels our friendship has to change. For whatever reason, we can no longer be friends. Knowing Earley, it's probably a good one. But I feel like I've lost the person I trusted the most. I know things don't stay the same, but I just want . . . I want to understand. I don't want to give up on him, Teresa. I don't want to lose your friendship either, but if the two of you keep acting like this, it's a forgone conclusion."

I glance at her to gage her reaction and realize she's looking a little taken aback by my directness. Her face is pale, and her spoon, so busy a few minutes before, is dangling sadly from her hand. Maybe she wasn't so ready for the truth after all.

"I don't know what to say. I didn't think our relationship would bother you so much, Lola. I thought you liked me, and you would be happy for us."

She stops and brings the hand with the ice cream container up to her forehead, so I can no longer see her expression; then she drops her hand with an almost inaudible breath and looks toward the sky.

"As for Earley, I can only guess at why he's acting the way he is," she continues. "In fact, I can probably make a pretty good guess, but I have to be careful not to say more, because I might be wrong."

"It doesn't have anything to do with 'liking' you." I make air quotes with my hand. "You know I like both of you, or I wouldn't be feeling so left out and lonely. Didn't you realize how much time I spent with Earley before you began dating?"

I suppress a groan. I can't believe I just admitted this to her. I have a question too, and I decide I'd better get it out of the way as well, because it's a distinct possibility. "I didn't do anything to offend either of you, did I?"

Teresa starts to laugh.

"No! I can almost guarantee you've done nothing. I have a feeling this is something that's entirely Earley. Okay, I'm guessing it might have something to do with what he would perceive as honorable boyfriend behavior." She chokes that one out through her laughter, but her mirth dies out as soon as she realizes I haven't joined her.

I don't think that's funny.

"Listen. I'll talk to Earley. All right? I can't promise a change, but I will. And Lola, I'm really sorry this has hurt you. I'm trying to be a better friend."

I nod.

And I try to shake off my melancholy. Isn't that what's expected?

Teresa and I continue to chat, munch, laugh, and be together, but it's a little hollow. It's only a temporary distraction from the sadness that's been lodged in the back of my throat for weeks. It's getting easier; I'm getting pretty good at pretending nothing's different; but a huge meteor struck and veered my life off course that day at lunch.

Maybe that was why it upset me so much, because I intuitively knew things would not be the same.

But more honestly, at that moment, I knew my relationship with Earley meant more than I had ever admitted to myself.

After all, all of my friends are valuable to me. I need Charlotte's honesty and loyalty; Teresa's kindness and good sense; Lauri's down-to-earth manner and invaluable laughter; and lately, George's companionship and sense of adventure.

But most of all, and more than anyone else, I need Earley. He's my defense when people attack me, he's my steady north star when the world seems upside down, and he's my family when no one else understands me. He's my unbreakable bank vault when secrets need to be shared, and he's my comfort when hugs are not to be found anywhere else on earth.

To heck with honorable boyfriend behavior, whatever that is.

Earley is . . . *was* . . . always right on time.

CHAPTER 14

We don't revisit the subject, but I guess Teresa spoke with Earley concerning our park conversation, because he loosens up. I don't have my friend completely back, but things are much better. He's not avoiding me, and he talks to me once more.

He's even correcting me again, which is a huge, rather surprising, comfort.

To be honest, I understand why we need to have a little more distance now. Teresa's his girlfriend, and I guess girlfriends come first, as much as it pains me to admit it.

And if I could pick any girlfriend for Earley (other than Pumpkin, of course. Um, that was a joke), I would pick Teresa.

In fact, things have improved so much he's beginning to hang out a little more at my house after school. Although I've noticed he makes sure Charlotte's around when he does. I guess he thinks we need a chaperone.

Go figure.

Then one day after Charlotte drops us off and drives away, much to my shock, he stops rather than charging straight down the street toward home. I'm guessing he needs to tie his shoe or something, and frankly, I feel no need to stick around and watch, so I turn to walk away.

"See ya, Earley." I head toward my door, then feel his hand on my arm. He's followed me down the walk a short way.

"Lola, hang on. Listen. My mom's been asking about you. Would you want to come over to dinner tonight and hang around a while?"

It's embarrassing, but I can't help but act like the sun has come out after a long, gray, snow-filled winter.

"Absolutely!" I reply with too much enthusiasm. But something about my answer must resonate with him, because he smiles his beautiful smile; then I can tell he's trying to be polite and hold back a laugh.

"All right. Okay then. Is 6:30 good?"

"Perfect," I respond while trying without much success to take my excitement down a notch or two.

"See ya later, Lola."

He turns and walks away as calm as can be. I rush inside the house, eager to start my homework for once.

Several hours later, my homework long since completed, I shout my good-byes to my parents and head out the door.

Dad follows me out onto the porch to watch me walk down the street.

"Wait, Lola. I want to talk to you for a second," he requests just as I launch myself off the top step.

"Sure." I walk back a few feet to face him.

"Is everything okay? I've noticed that, until tonight, you haven't been at Earley and Grace's house in several weeks." I'm surprised he's noticed. Raised on a farm and with a faded barbed-wire scar across his cheek as evidence, he's a typical no-nonsense engineer. He doesn't appear to take in or comment much on my doings, seemingly oblivious. And Mom has been too busy with her new career and placing my grandmother, recently diagnosed with Alzheimer's, in a nursing home to pay real attention. I'm actually okay with that—I don't want to worry them.

"Well, Earley is dating Teresa now, and . . ."

I'm not sure what else to say, so I finish with a shrug.

This is clearly outside of his comfort zone. "Oh . . . well, I want you to know if there's anything bothering you, you can let your mom and I know. Okay?" he concludes in his bass tones.

I nod in response, step up, and give him a hug.

"We're on your side," he murmurs into my hair. I'm not sure I fully comprehend the depth of his words, but maybe this is something I didn't know I needed to hear until he said it. I let out a breath that I just might have been holding for months.

"I love you, Dad."

"I love you, too, Lola."

I turn to trot down the hill to Earley and Grace's house, my fluffy brown hair bouncing around my face, trying to absorb the impact of Dad's words as I walk away. Is this a good thing or a bad thing that's he's been paying more attention than I thought? Possibly good, but I feel a bit unsettled by it nevertheless. At the corner, I turn back to see if he's still on the porch and catch the movement of the door closing behind him.

He stood there a lot longer than necessary.

I cross the street to step into their yard, arriving at their porch in another half-second, but just as I raise my finger to ring the doorbell, I become a bit nervous and shy. I haven't seen Grace in so long.

I gather my courage and press the button to catch its faint chiming through the door.

I hear muffled mutterings as footsteps approach the entry; then a backlit Earley appears before me, long and lanky, a dusk blue shadow. Stunning.

Just looking at him makes my chest ache.

"Hey. Come on in," he greets me and steps back. I shake my head to clear it as I walk across the sill.

He closes the door behind me, steps around, and motions for me to follow him back to the kitchen.

As we walk I hear loud music and even louder singing. Unreserved, and with joy as her evident companion, Grace is playing the Beatles and crooning. I didn't hear the music through the door, but now I know why she didn't answer my ring as she usually does.

We walk into the den/kitchen combo, and she's so startled by our approach, she drops the head of lettuce she's holding. It bounces from the countertop to the floor and rolls toward our feet, all to the accompaniment of "The Long and Winding Road." Earley acts as if he's going to kick it, but Grace makes a hurried noise of objection and rushes around the countertop to retrieve it from where it rests in front of us.

She stoops down, grabs the lettuce, places it under one arm, straightens, and grabs me with the other.

I shouldn't be surprised, but she squeezes me as if she hasn't seen me in a year.

I return the hug with enthusiasm, and the ache within my chest loosens its embrace.

I love Grace.

She gives the best hugs, and she gives them often.

I think she's the reason Earley was always so comfortable with my affection up until recently.

She grabs my hand as if I would bolt at any moment, then pulls me into the kitchen where she turns down the volume, talking all the while and bombarding me with question after question.

When we sit down to eat a little while later, they don't know it, but I stifle tears of gratitude to God. It's sweet to watch them interact. It's so *sweet* to feel, at least for a while, as if I'm a part of it.

Somehow Grace must sense my mood, because she looks over at me and says, "It's so good you're here, my sweet Lola."

It almost feels like home.

Things have changed, but for a time . . . for a few more minutes . . . I can pretend Earley is still the most important person in my life, even if I'm not the most important in his.

I guess if I'm forced to put Earley into the back seat of my life, my consolation prize is George. And to be honest, he's much better (and better looking) than any other consolation prize I could've dreamed up.

Like Lauri and me, George is funny in a kind of wicked way—the three of us are always cracking up over our own jokes at lunch.

I've stopped sitting next to Earley, by the way. I came into lunch one day and found Lauri in my spot. But I decided it was for the best. After all, George still sits across from us, and this gives the three of us ample opportunity to cut up.

George seems to love to tease me, but I give it right back. Charlotte and Lauri cheer me on, Jack eggs George on, Teresa and

Earley try to referee, and Pumpkin sits and smiles at our antics. Jeff and Annie don't pay us much attention.

"Lola, my dad's angry with you," George says with a straight face while dropping his tray down on the Formica table, oblivious to his carton of milk bouncing off onto the tabletop.

I reach to straighten and place it back on his tray as I puzzle out his proclamation.

"What? What did I do?"

"You threw your beer cans in our yard last night; he wants you to clean them up pronto," he continues but starts laughing toward the end.

I give him a *look*. "I wasn't the scumbag who threw those cans in his yard last night, but I can point him in the right direction."

"Oh yeah? And which direction would that be?" he smirks.

"As the saying goes, he needs to start at home." I quirk an eyebrow; then I feel my lips start to turn up in an answering smirk.

George begins to laugh but regains his straight face.

"Are you accusing my *dad* of throwing beer cans into his *own* yard?" His tone is self-righteous, but his smile is all mischief.

Our laughter reverberates around the cafeteria, but while I'm trying to think of a way to top that one, I get sidetracked. Strange noises emanate from Pumpkin's vicinity. Funny enough, she's so overcome with laughter she's holding her middle, swaying back and forth, and . . . is she snorting? This is so uncharacteristic that she's silenced the rest of the table.

She soon notices the quiet, because she stops, looking self-conscious. Then we all begin laughing again, and she honks back in.

Lunch ends before I can think of the perfect response to George's kidding, but I'm not worried. I'll have plenty of time to get him back tomorrow. The thought makes me smile as I walk toward my next class.

As I turn to leave my locker for the parking lot at the end of the day, I find three angry girls blocking my path—Michelle, Kim, and one of their friends.

I try to walk around them, but whenever I take a step in one direction, one of them steps into my path to cut me off.

"Gee whiz. Let me by," I give in enough to remark. Besides, their friend is even taller and more muscular than Michelle. Dang it. I mean, I think she's a girl, but she could be a guy with a delicate face who wears skirts.

"We told you to stay away from George, but you were too much of a moron to listen," Kim sneers.

Are they serious? Michelle and George aren't even dating anymore! "We're just friends."

"*We're just friends*," Kim mimics.

"Liar!" Michelle snarls. "I've seen you with him, slut. You flirt constantly. You're the reason he broke up with me."

"I don't know what you're talking about. Back up!"

But they just keep getting closer and closer until they're right in my face.

I feel like I can't breathe.

Can't think.

I can't take it!

"Back up!" I yell again, but they don't seem to hear or care; then I see the biggest girl ball her hand into a fist and draw back her elbow as if in slow motion. It looks like she knows how to hit, and her fist is aimed at my stomach as if there's a big bull's-eye on it.

On reflex, I cross my hands over my middle, hunch down, and head butt my way out the opposite side of the circle. The blow never lands. I hear a crash behind me as if something has rammed the locker, and I whirl around to see a dent in the metal.

The girl screams in pain, cradling her fist to her chest.

"Grab her, Michelle!" Kim shrieks. I see that Michelle's about to follow Kim's urging, so I run like lightning toward the stairs. I'm not going to let them corner me again!

As I skid to grab the bannister at the top of the stairs, I see George on the landing below and remember he was going to meet me at my locker after school. Disregarding the present peril for the previous one, I leap down toward him, spinning around once I reach the landing to look back up.

"Lola, what's wrong?"

Michelle and Kim have paused at the top of the staircase with twin looks of horror on their faces.

"George, I . . . *huff, huff* . . . can't take it . . . *huff* . . . anymore. Please tell your violent former girlfriend that you didn't break up with her because of me. She's crazy," I manage to get out between pants.

An ominous pause ensues.

George stares up at the landing. I've never seen his face so dark. "I don't have to repeat it. She knows why I broke up with her. She messed around with another guy. And she's crazy as well as stupid

if she's trying to hurt you. She knows that anyone that threatens you will have to deal with me. *And* Pumpkin. Let's go."
He's looking directly at Michelle as he speaks.
"*What?* You didn't tell me that!" Kim accuses Michelle.
"Aaaaargh! I was trying to make him jealous! It was *her* fault!"
Michelle crumples down onto the top step and starts up some of the loudest bawling I've ever heard.
She's acting like an oversized baby.
I can't watch. I'm starting to feel a little sick on top of overwhelmed by my desire to get away, so I follow George as he reverses course toward the parking lot.
He doesn't look back once.

I find out later that their friend, Ramona, broke two bones in her hand punching my locker. But the punishment didn't stop there. George reported their attack to the principal with the result that they've all received three-day suspensions, and Kim and Michelle are no longer cheerleaders.
My parents are not taking this well. They've started wondering whether or not Sunset is a safe place for me. I hope they're soon distracted, because that was just the result I feared. It's one of the reasons I don't tell them much. After all, I don't want to be separated from my friends.
I'm guessing (okay, hoping) those girls will leave me alone from now on.

Over the next several weeks, I get so comfortable around George that I forget he's not Earley. I even forget he's student body president and captain of the football team. It's like a miracle. I don't mean I start calling him by the wrong name or anything. I mean he becomes fully George to me, or just George.

Yep. Despite his undiminished good looks, he's no longer George the Gorgeous.

I even start asking him about his weekend plans, and I always include him in our group's activities.

Then, without much thought, we start making plans for just the two of us. We go to new restaurants, and we shop together.

Basically, we roam Dallas.

We're true friends, but we're not dating. There's no kissing involved, but there's some affection nevertheless. Besides, I'm okay with the status quo. Believe it or not.

After all, it's George. I can't imagine he would ever be interested in more with me.

"Shhh! Stop laughing. Be quiet!" George hisses, but I continue to shake; I know at any moment I'm going to burst out laughing.

Then he pinches me on the arm.

That sobers me up.

"Ow," I whisper.

"Sorry, but you're going to give us away," he apologizes and then rubs the spot on my arm where he pinched me.

"You can pinch me again if that's my recompense," I encourage with an arch smile. He raises his eyebrows and smirks.

"Hmmm. Well, I'm still sorry, but you've got to be quiet," he reiterates and then mutters something under his breath about his dad, Henry, killing him if he ever finds out that George pinched me. I'm wondering why he isn't worried about his dad finding out about our prank, but then I think better of it.

Most adults would understand our need for a laugh at the expense of the Demented Duo. George understands, anyway. In fact, it was his suggestion. He's been dying to get back at them ever since Matthew said those awful things about me in front of him.

We're spying on Matthew (Luke is nowhere to be found), but it really doesn't matter whether one or both are pranked.

They're practically the same person after all, just like Turdley.

It's after school on a Friday in December. George is between sports seasons, so he doesn't have to be anywhere right now. Most of the students have already left, but for some reason, Matthew is loitering around, kissing and feeling up his girlfriend; he doesn't seem in any hurry to open his locker.

"Yuck. He's gross. How can she go out with him?" I whisper in a voice laced with disbelief.

George snickers and pulls me further back behind the column we're hiding behind. "I really can't say, but I want them to, ah, conclude, so we can see his reaction when he opens the locker."

"I know. I feel like a voyeur."

"Unfortunately, at this point, I don't think you could classify our actions as anything other than voyeuristic," he says and rolls his eyes at me.

"Okay, okay, but it'll all be worth it when he opens it."

As we're whispering back and forth, they finally say their good-byes, and she walks off as he turns back to his locker.

My anticipation mounts. He's lifting the catch but it's stuck, so he gives it several rough jiggles. The Duo feel no need to place locks on their lockers. Who would dare to trespass on them? It's now my turn to grab George's arm and squeeze a little too hard in my excitement.

Matthew opens the door.

A supporting piece of cardboard and what must be a trillion and a half dried green peas come crashing out of the tight space and rush over him in a chartreuse wave before he has a chance to scramble out of the way; a large poster unfolds from the door where it's been mounted.

"You could use more than one IQ point," the sign reads.

He shouts in alarm, giving a standard one-syllable swear word four syllables for extra emphasis; and then all kinds of loud, creative obscenities follow in its wake to the light accompaniment of peas skittering and scattering down the hall.

We look at each other, faces scrunched up with gleeful, over-the-top expressions. "Oops. I'll bet that'll take some time to clean up," I comment with zero remorse.

"It worked better than I thought it would. He *is* a pea brain." George states the obvious.

He grabs my hand and pulls me down the hall. He soon lets go, and we run toward the parking lot.

We make it to the car and fumble our way in; then George starts it up.

As we're driving out of the lot, we see Matthew running out of the school with the sign trailing out of his hand. Before we turn the next corner, effectively blocking our view of the school, I see him ball the sign up, throw it to the ground, and stomp on it with vigor.

He looks angry in the extreme, making our happiness complete.

And our luck only gets better—there are still several cars in the lot, so he can't prove it was us.

The joke is goofy, as are all practical jokes, so I apologize for that, but suffice it to say, Matthew and Luke more than deserve it.

As George drives away, we congratulate each other on our success.

Vengeance is so, so sweet.

What's the cherry on top? We hear on Monday that the vice principal blamed the Demented Duo for the mess. He accused them of trying to hatch a prank! Matthew must've destroyed or thrown away the sign and can't prove their innocence. They're forced to stay after school every afternoon for a week to help the custodial staff clean the cafeteria as punishment.

I just have to comment: life is better with George around. I haven't been tempted to curse or name call in weeks. I mean, who cares about getting rid of Matthew and Luke when they're effectively rendered impotent by my friendship with our resident superhero?

CHAPTER 15

We had so much fun that George and I decide to continue our pranking spree and recruit some of our other friends for our next ingenious (and more ambitious) adventure.

It's the first Saturday night of the winter semester, and we're headed to north Dallas.

George is driving. I'm riding shotgun. Jack, Lauri, and Charlotte are crammed in the back. But just as I'm starting to feel a little guilty for calling the front seat, Jack starts complaining about how tight the fit is between the two cute girls he's between. All my sympathy leaks out my slightly open window.

"C'mon, Jack. You know you have the best seat in the house," George chides.

"Hmmf!" Jack responds as we continue past downtown and toward University Park.

I twist my body to glance into the back seat. I could've guessed, but Jack has his arms crossed in front of his chest and a recalcitrant set to his jaw. Charlotte and Lauri give each other looks with raised eyebrows across the car, only to simultaneously turn away to look out the window and ignore Jack's atypical rudeness.

I decide to follow their good example and focus back toward the windshield.

We're headed for the Southern Methodist University campus, because I've got a devious idea that is brilliant in its simplicity.

As I may have already mentioned, in our city, anything north of downtown is automatically considered somehow better than anything south. Many of the North Dallas residents wouldn't dream of setting foot in Oak Cliff. They're afraid of heading into an unsafe and unsavory neighborhood. We've decided, therefore, to spread a little of our Oak Cliff affection into the north, and we hope we're stealthy enough to avoid detection.

"Jack, I *promise* we won't get caught," I assure him. I know behind his grumpiness is a reasonable concern that what we're about to do could get us in big-time trouble.

"You cannot promise that, Lo-luh," he softly singsongs, but I continue to ignore his cranky attitude.

"You brought the bumper stickers, right?" I continue.

Fortunately for us, Jack's mom works at the Oak Cliff Chamber of Commerce, and his assistance is invaluable in tonight's little escapade. In truth, I'm not sure why he's worried; his mother's in on the plan. He didn't spell it out for her, but she provided all seventy-five bumper stickers. I'm sorry, but teens don't gather that many of any object without some kind of sneaky ulterior motive.

We exit the freeway at Mockingbird and take a left, passing Mrs. Baird's Bakery on the way. I'm glad the window's cracked; it usually smells like fresh-baked bread at this intersection.

"Getting high on the bread fumes, bobcat?" George teases when he notices me taking in a huge whiff of the yeast-scented air.

"You got it." I don't see any reason to deny it.

Just to give you a little background: Southern Methodist University, founded in 1911, is situated among the upper-crust neighborhoods of University and Highland Parks. In other words, it's smack dab in the middle of Dallas. As we drive around the periphery of the campus we pass sweet, pristine gems of houses situated in between bigger, statelier homes.

Everyone's lawns are well kept.

Everything is well kept. I don't think they allow even the smallest gum wrapper to rest for long on their immaculate sidewalks, which is, actually, a bit of a problem for us. The University Park and campus police probably have nothing better to do than drink coffee, help open doors for little old ladies who lock themselves out, and chase down a few drunken but still orderly frat boys on a given Saturday night.

We find a parking spot at Snider Plaza, a surprisingly normal (i.e., unsophisticated) shopping center for the neighborhood and nearby the campus. It houses Hudson's, a burger joint, which has red-and-white checked sticky plastic tablecloths and big windows from which we can view the car.

We pull ourselves from the vehicle; the slamming of the car doors clunks with unnatural loudness.

We try to be unobtrusive as we amble down a few blocks toward a streetlight with a crosswalk; then Charlotte bumps into Lauri, almost knocking her from the narrow sidewalk into the street in front of a car. George, fast as a striking snake, manages to grab Lauri by the arm and pull her back to the middle of the pavement.

The close call gives me an adrenaline rush; I place my hand on my chest and feel my heart pound away as I try to get my panic under control.

I look around. In tune with my rushing heart, Lauri's almost panting, and Charlotte has her hands raised and over her eyes. Jack's scowl has deepened to alarming proportions. I'm not sure if that crease will ever come out of his forehead.

Only George looks unfazed—his eyes are bright with purpose—he's keeping us on track.

So we, in silent agreement, give ourselves a few moments to recover our composure and continue on our way.

The little green walking man flashes; we quickly cross the street with his help, our eyes darting here and there in the hope we're not being noticed.

As soon as we're across, we saunter under and are swallowed by the dark canopy of trees surrounding the university grounds. But before we can emerge from them into a world of burnt-umber brick buildings and ultimate preppiness, George calls us to stop.

"Huddle up. Okay, here's the plan."

"George, we've already discussed this," I whine and roll my eyes.

"Hush, woman. We need to go over it one more time. Okay—c'mon, Lola, don't interrupt me again—if we get caught, remember to scatter and get off campus as quickly as possible before making your way back to the restaurant, finding a secluded place to pull off your disguise beforehand. Don't hover around the car, but go into Hudson's and order a drink or some food. Find a table with a view of it . . . the car, I mean. Those who arrive first will wait until midnight for any who've not shown up, then start calling parents."

I hear Jack give a quiet moan at about the same time that I feel myself give an involuntary cringe, but we all nod our heads in agreement.

I guess we're in.

"Break!" George adds as a joke.

Oh, brother.

But he's right. It's good to be prepared. As he mentioned, we even have disguises of sorts. Our camouflage of choice is dark sweaters, jackets, or coats that can be easily removed after our work is complete.

"Remember to keep up with our trash, guys," I remind them in a stage whisper as we begin to move again. "We don't want to leave a trail of breadcrumbs for anyone to follow."

I hear a few nervous snickers and quiet whispers as we quickly pass the music building. It's not long before we emerge at the edge of the center of the grounds, so we pause to scope out possible areas of infiltration. We see dorms across the way, realize the likelihood of large parking lots close by, and start a zigzag course across the open space in the middle of the campus.

Fortunately for us, the mall area is interspersed with trees, providing continued cover as we move like wraiths toward our goal.

At least, we imagine we're moving like wraiths.

Our targeted dorms are situated in a U-shape around a grassy area, and we keep walking until we're sneaking behind the bottom of the U. We see a small stadium and realize we've hit pay dirt.

There are resident parking lots close by.

So we get to work. We go from BMW to Mercedes to BMW (huh—there's a Toyota), laboring with diligence to spread our Oak Cliff devotion but making sure to clean up after ourselves as if we're good little SMU students. From time to time, people walk out and start up their cars or cross the lot headed somewhere else on campus, but no one approaches closely.

No one seems to suspect we're up to no good.

Charlotte is our lookout, and when she signals a presence we stop our work and mill about as if we're on our way in or out of campus and have stopped for a chat.

"Focus, guys! We can do this!" George encourages in a whisper.

"I can't believe we *are* doing this," Charlotte states with a quiet chuckle.

"Hi-ho, hi-ho . . . it's off to ruin we go," Jack softly sings.

"My hands are shaking so badly, I can't peel the backing off the stickers," Lauri murmurs.

"Jack, stop singing that! It's making me laugh!" I hiss out.

"Well, gosh, that's an unusual request, but *o-kaaay*," he replies.

We cover fifty or so cars when our luck runs out.

George tells us to play it cool as a campus policeman patrolling in a golf cart decides to pull up to see why we're loitering or give us a friendly warning and a "Move along, Mustangs." But he must have keen powers of observation, because as soon as he stops, his eyes dart down and along the bumpers of the cars surrounding us and almost comically bug out.

"Wha? What are you *doin*?" He jumps out of his cart with surprising agility for his plump size and grabs me, the closest, by the arm while the rest of the group scatters . . . except Jack, who seems frozen in place.

Yes, Jack's a bug caught in the beam of a powerful flashlight. I mouth at him to run, but he seems in a fear trance.

"Stay where you are!" the policeman yells at him, but it's a waste of breath. Jack's not going anywhere.

I think our new friend finally realizes Jack's state, because he takes my bag and proceeds to cuff my hands behind my back, temporarily leaving my coconspirator unattended.

By the way, why is he restraining me? Do I look particularly dangerous? I don't feel dangerous.

Strange enough, the cop seems nervous. His keys jingle like the bells on a Christmas sleigh harness as he works on the handcuffs.

His walkie-talkie, squawking and hissing, adds to the dissonant symphony. A scratchy voice demanding to speak to Officer Wilson emanates from it. I hear him mutter something like "hold your horses" under his breath as he's tightening the restraints.

"Ow," I mouth in surprise. The cuffs are too tight, but I don't want to voice my complaint, because it might backfire on me.

Meanwhile, Jack must be having a panic attack because he's not made a peep. I'm not sure he's even breathing.

I hope he doesn't pass out.

The policeman proceeds to manhandle me into the golf cart as if I'm a hardened criminal; then he dumps my bag on the front seat. *Clunk.* Next, as if he senses Jack is about to lose it, he gently escorts Jack over and eases him into the seat beside me ("Easy there, son"), not even bothering to restrain him.

Unacknowledged buzzing continues from the walkie-talkie.

"So you're from Oak Cliff, huh?" the campus policeman states in a shaky voice.

I don't think he expects a response.

The cuffs continue to jingle-jingle as we take off across campus, bumping over speed bumps and minor potholes, giving my thoughts time to catch up with our predicament. I didn't think we'd be caught, much less cuffed if we were! My shock at the manhandling is beginning to wear off, and I feel myself becoming overwhelmed by the enormity of our situation. My parents may blow a gasket over this, either about the prank itself, the unnecessary cuffing, or both.

Out of the blue, we hit a bad bump. Panic once again surges through my system as I feel myself begin to tumble out of the cart, only to be saved by an unexpected hand on my arm, pulling me back upright.

It's Jack, and he's awake!

He winks at me, causing me to realize he's been putting on a bit of show for the benefit of our captor. *Whew!* Feelings of relief temporarily overpower some of the other emotions knocking around inside of me.

Within minutes, we pull up to the campus police headquarters, a small building at the edge of campus. The walkie-talkie squawks out another warning just as we arrive. The voice on the other end insists on the owner's assistance at a frat party on the other side of the university grounds. The gathering is getting a little loud or something bordering on unmanageable, I guess.

Heaven forbid.

Pszzz! Crackle! Pszzz!

"Come in, Officer Wilson. I repeat—your *immediate* assistance is needed at the Phi house," the person on the other end blasts out.

Two crimes at once must be more than our host can handle because he seems even more discombobulated now. He begins his response only to be cut off and told to get over to fraternity row pronto.

"Gee whiz! Enough already! Okay, I'll be there as soon as I can." He's not only irritable but unprofessional as well.

The officer pushes us into the little anteroom of the office, plunks my bag on a desk behind the counter, and tells us to stay as if we're two disobedient dogs he needs to get in hand.

We mutely nod our heads as he walks back out into the night, but almost as soon as the door whooshes shut, Jack turns to me.

"Don't worry, Lola. We must've thrown him way off balance. He left the keys in the cuffs, believe it or not. I mean, how stupid can you get? I'll have them off in a jiffy."

I guess it's not a surprise that it seems to take more than a *jiffy* due to his lack of experience, but Jack does remove the cuffs. They clink and clatter to the floor, and we leave them where they fall.

I lean over the counter to snag my bag, and we rush out of the building. Once at the outer edge of campus, we look around for potential witnesses. When no one seems near, Jack pulls off his black cap and windbreaker while I yank out my ponytail holder, removing what feels like half my hair in my haste. I then fling off my navy peacoat, revealing the pastel blue sweater underneath.

Only then do we stop to breathe.

"Lola, you *promised* we wouldn't get caught!" Jack, trying to catch his breath, accuses me in jest. My response is to laugh so hard I double over, then sit down on the grass for a minute to try to regain my calm; my head quickly ends up between my knees. I can't believe I was responsible for that. In fact, I think I may be a tad hysterical.

Yep, my hands are shaking.

"I'm . . . *so* sorry. I'm so glad you didn't run away. I would still be sitting there. And I'm pretty sure my parents wouldn't be as understanding as your mom. Thank you, Jack." My voice sounds as wobbly as my still-quaking hands and heart.

"Yeah, you'd be in the only stuffy little building north of downtown with no circulation in your hands," he replies. Then he pauses before he continues in a more serious voice, "To be honest, I was too surprised to run at first, but I felt I had to stay once everyone else scattered. And speaking of everyone else, we better get back to the car before they call a parent."

I take a deep breath and stand up a little unsteadily, and we begin weaving our way back to the meeting place.

We spot our friends sitting around a table framed by a huge window. They seem to be having a serious discussion.

They don't see us until we enter, causing a bell to jingle over the door. The place is fairly crowded, but within seconds, I'm enveloped in a huge hug.

I'm a little bemused to find I'm held so tightly that I can't see who has me, but I'm able to smell the person, making identification a cinch.

It's George and his wonderful George smell.

He's smoothing down my hair, and frankly, he has me in a death grip. It makes breathing a bit difficult, but I somehow manage to get the olfactory clue despite not being able to see past the cotton shirt approximately two millimeters from my eyes.

Of course, the upside is getting attention from George.

Then I realize he's saying something over and over again, and it sounds like he's saying he's sorry.

He lets me go, and I'm finally able to stand back to look at him.

"You don't have to apologize. We're fine. See?" I reply, but my face heats up, and I decide to pull my sleeves down to hide the fading red rings where I was cuffed.

It's only moments before Lauri and Charlotte crowd around, pushing us farther apart. It's funny, because they're patting Jack and me on the back, arms, and head as if they're checking for lost parts. Blessedly, the pat-down doesn't last long; then they start in with questions, but just as Jack and I begin to answer, we're interrupted.

"Wait. We need to get out of here. We need to get home." George displays some wisdom.

"Oh, man. Definitely. I don't want to run across that campus policeman again, ever, in my lifetime," I croak out.

With relief, we pile back into George's car, but I let Jack sit in the front as his reward for being the conquering hero.

He accepts his prize with great aplomb; then we're on our way back home . . . back to Oak Cliff where we belong.

The next morning as I stumble into the kitchen to see what's for breakfast, the usual scene greets me: my parents sitting at our breakfast bar absentmindedly eating while they peruse the paper.

I sit down, but as I start to butter my toast, I notice the paper next to me start to shake.

"Dave, what's going on? Why are you *shaking?*" my mother asks with concern.

Huge, unexpected guffaws emanate from within the paper; then my sedate, serious father drops it on the floor.

And we realize he's unable to answer because he's laughing too hard.

After a few seconds he manages to pick up the newspaper and hold it out to my mother while pointing at an article, all the while trying to control his mirth and catch his breath.

She has a quizzical look on her face but takes it and begins to read the article out loud.

"Okay . . . hmmm . . . blah, blah. Okay . . . here's the relevant part, I think. 'Several student cars were vandalized on the Southern Methodist University campus yesterday evening. Fred Wilson, long-time campus policeman, reports he interrupted approximately seven young people in the act of unlawfully planting "I heart Oak Cliff" stickers on cars parked behind one of the dorms. He reports over sixty-five cars were plastered with stickers.' Oh, my! And they got away!" She starts laughing as well.

I try to project innocence with an anemic smile and a fake laugh, but I'm not sure I'm cutting it, because my mom suddenly looks at me with a shrewd, parental look.

"Lola, where were you and your friends last night? Did you have fun?"

"Oh, sure. We went to eat at Tachito's," I mumble and then stick about half a piece of toast in my mouth so I won't have to say anything else. And technically, I'm not lying—we did eat at Tachito's before heading across town.

She continues to look at me with suspicion.

"Doesn't Jack's mother work at the Oak Cliff Chamber of Commerce? I think they pass out bumper stickers like that."

Yep, my breakfast is over.

I swallow down my toast blob without choking, ask to be excused, and scurry from the room.

I can't believe we made the paper.

I'm never doing anything like that again.

Never, ever.

My parents found out. My mom is too clever by half. She and Jack's mom conferred and connected the dots after Mom discovered a few of the leftover bumper stickers under some clothes at the bottom of my closet.

My parents called the campus police and turned me in. Their own daughter. It's outrageous!

Although I suppose I'm getting off pretty lightly. I'm glad that they didn't make a big deal about me not naming the other culprits. Most of the owners of the cars have already scraped off the stickers, so my punishment consists of washing the ten or so campus police vehicles next Saturday morning.

I guess I'll live.

I realize I have the best friends in the world when George, Jack, and Pumpkin show up to help me scrub golf carts.

We make sure to leave the campus police a few bumper stickers on the counter in case they feel the need to decorate their vehicles after we're gone.

CHAPTER 16

When Monday rolls around, we're talking and laughing about our escapades around the lunch table. Pumpkin had a cousin's birthday party to attend; Teresa, Earley, Jeff, and Annie were on a double date, so they missed out.

It doesn't, however, keep them from teasing, chastising, and congratulating us by turns.

"Why didn't you run when you first saw the security guard?" Earley accuses with a pointed look at George.

George cocks an eyebrow at him, then turns toward Jack, essentially ignoring Earley's question. Probably for the best. Personally, I think George made the only decision he could've at the spur of the moment. After all, we're not all athletes like him and Earley. Yes, the majority of us ended up running anyway, but George was trying to avoid that. If one of us had been hurt while attempting to get away, it would have been an even bigger problem than my irritated parents picking up my mischievous self at the campus police station.

Back on track, I'm observing something even more interesting at our table than Earley's interrogation tactics. Jack, our hero du jour, sits tall. It's a bit of a surprise, but he's become our unofficial storyteller, and he's definitely feeling good about his part in my getaway, as he should. Pumpkin, moreover, seems to hang on to his every word and find him particularly funny.

It's cute to see her so engaged and entertained by our adventure. She looks even prettier than usual as she snorts at all the appropriate places.

Confidentially, it's nice to know she snorts when she laughs. It makes her seem more human.

The bell rings to signal that it's time for class, so we throw away the last of our trash and start toward the swinging purple doors.

"Lola, wait!" George calls out.

I turn to look around, but I can't seem to locate him in the mashing, mixing mass of students.

Then I spot him; he's closer than I realized.

"What's up, buddy?" I ask as he deftly emerges from the now thinning crowd.

"Don't call me buddy."

"I won't as long as you never ever call me 'woman' again."

"Ha! Listen. Would you like to grab some ice cream after school? We can run by Polar Bear over by Lake Cliff. What do you think?"

"Sounds good. My mom'll be at her real estate classes until dinnertime, so she won't be wondering where I am. I'll let Charlotte know I'm riding home with you. Okay?"

"Oh-kay!" He claps his hands, then rubs them together as if he's rather excited about something.

I'm a little mystified and a little amused, because he seems the epitome of chipper and I don't know why. I don't have time to remark on it before he winks at me, a definite distraction.

"Get to class, woman." He gives me a stern look and turns to walk away.

"Hey! Stop calling me that!" I call after him. He looks over his shoulder, winks again, and gives me a thumbs up to acknowledge my parting words.

After school, I walk to the edge of the parking lot and stop.

A little way off, I see a sunglasses-clad George lounging against his car's windshield with his feet on the hood and his face to the sky.

I'm pretty sure he hasn't noticed me.

Girls walk past. The shy ones briefly glance and look away. The bold ones give him a once-over, a loud hello, and maybe even a leer. The friendly ones look over, their expressions softening, before giving him a confident greeting and continuing on their way.

He greets them in turn and even turns to stare after a few as they walk past—so typical, and a sure warning I should be careful with my heart. After all, George would never stare after me.

In a way, I'm glad.

Friendship is best.

Stares are trivial.

Stares are *nothing*.

I walk out a few more steps and wait. I now see his eyes closed beneath his glasses. His long, brown eyelashes make a soft smile across the top of his cheeks.

I still think he's gorgeous, but I'll never tell him.

So I shake off my contemplative mood, and quiet as a mouse, I continue forward.

But just before I reach the car I decide to give him a good scare to shake things up a bit.

"Boo!" I shout as I bang my hand down on the hood of his car. He startles, but not to the extent I expect.

"Hey! Hands off the car, bobcat! I saw you sneaking up on me. What do you think you are? A spy? I'm going to start calling you the spymeister; you've got sneaky ways. Not," he taunts as he hops off the car. Then he pulls me over to give me what I think will be a hug, only to flip me around and ruffle my hair for good measure.

It's my turn to protest.

"Stop it, George!" I demand and give him an elbow to the gut.

"*Oof!* Only if you agree to be my slave and serve me as I should be served. I am, after all, a god."

"Oh brother," I mumble as I wiggle away and reach to open the passenger-side door of his car.

He jogs to the driver's side, opens the door, and slides into his seat, as graceful as the athlete he is.

It's January, by the way, but we're having a balmy day; the temperature has reached the high sixties. The car is warm inside, so we roll down the windows and crank the eight-track. As we drive, the wind is blowing through my hair; I'm sure I look like a tangled mess. I don't care for once, but I decide to grab my hair and hold it in a loose ponytail to keep it out of my face.

We make the trip to Polar Bear in its white overly-stuccoed glory across from Lake Cliff Park, because ice cream is on the agenda. We both get two scoops, and he teases me about eating as much as he does, but he pays. That's a nice treat.

"Thanks," I say.

"Of course," he matter-of-factly responds. I find it a strange reply but don't feel like breaking the mood with trivial questions, so I leave it alone.

George suggests we head to the park to eat our ice cream. We cross the busy street with caution. He's always very aware of his surroundings, and he knows I can sometimes be absentminded; he usually makes sure I'm alert when we're together and need to be careful. In anyone else I would find it officious, but it's George, so it doesn't bother me.

We eat our ice cream and walk around the lake, then head to the playground where there's a super tall rocket slide. We sit on one of the brightly painted nearby benches, and I tell George stories about how scared I was to climb the slide as a small child but worked up the nerve because I didn't want to be left behind when Elizabeth played on it.

As we're reminiscing, he decides it's time to call me "Robin" to kid me about our preschool antics—he, Elizabeth, and I would don kitchen aprons and pretend to be the Caped Crusader and his sidekicks. As the youngest, I was almost always relegated to playing Robin.

They're great memories. So I let him get away with one more nickname with a minimum of protest.

"I can't believe you almost fell through the church's ceiling. What in the world were you doing up there? And even more important, did your parents know where you were?" I shake my head in incredulity at the series of close-call stories George recounts.

"No! Are you kidding me? My mom would've had a cow. It would not have been pretty." He gives a rueful chuckle; then it's his turn to shake his head in disbelief.

A while later the sun begins its quick winter descent, and the air starts to turn chilly. George pulls me over, and I sit within the crook of his arm to stay warm.

We're quiet as we watch the few remaining children play; then our vision broadens, and we look over past the lake as the lights of downtown begin to shimmer out of the dulling day.

Finally, it's dusk. Everything's a deep, rich blue . . . the lake, the air, the buildings and the grass. In the near distance, blue-black, bare tree branches punctuate the air closer to the ground, giving it texture and character. Bright and brighter pinpricks of white continue to twinkle on across the Trinity River. And the children leave with their parents to head to warmer venues.

Their sweet, high-pitched, songlike voices grow quieter and quieter as they walk toward their cars.

But George and I continue to sit. We talk off and on, but we're very relaxed and feel no need to hurry.

"Lola, do you *really* believe in God?" George asks out of nowhere.

"Yeah. Don't you?" I respond in surprise.

"Yes, especially now. I feel very thankful right now. I feel thankful to have you in my life. You're a good person. Sometimes . . . sometimes I think I would do . . . anything for you. I really like you, Lola," he discloses with a tiny note of surprise in his voice.

I still on instinct.

I'm trying to process his words; then I'm overwhelmed by their weight, but I don't want to show it.

He doesn't mean what he's saying, after all.

He doesn't realize how he *sounds*.

But being robbed of the brief feeling of hope he's given feels like something bordering on despair.

My body feels as if it's shrinking . . . as if it's turning in on itself . . . but I *have* to cage my emotions, because they've always been a little wild.

They've never been my friends.

Yet the effort to respond with even a semblance of normalcy seems so phenomenal, it feels as if I'm killing a rather large piece of myself.

"Thanks. I think you're pretty great too. I'm so, *so* glad you're my friend," I scrape out and clear my throat of the knot stuck in it; then I gather enough bravery (just enough) to pull away to look toward his familiar face.

His look seems to say I could do better.

I shrug my shoulders and give him a weak smile, but I'm not sure what to add or share.

Earley cured me of sharing too much.

George looks off into the distance, away from me, while simultaneously pulling me a little tighter against him. The move forces me to turn away from him.

"Of course you do. I am, after all, *me*," he says with what could possibly be a tinge of self-mockery. I feel him shrug off my insufficiency while muttering under his breath.

I think I catch Earley's name.

I'm not sure.

And I'm definitely not sure how to respond, so I reply with a pathetic, fake little huff and a shake of the head. Then I stand up and grab his hand to pull him from the bench.

I feel the need to continue to pull him all the way back to the car, so I never let go of his hand.

CHAPTER 17

The next week holds all the standard teenage ups and downs, but it's a bit heavier on the downs because of the Demented Duo.

Matthew and Luke seem even more bold and angry than usual. I'm not sure what's happened to cause an increase in their ire, but I've heard a rumor about the consequences.

People say Matthew's been hitting his girlfriend.

I wish I had the nerve to tell her she could do about a gajillion times better than a worm like him, but I don't know her at all, so my words go unsaid.

Anyway, they've started to harass me again, albeit not in George's presence.

"You're such a slut. I bet you give it out to George all the time." None of the adults seem to hear or care. As for the students, they're afraid that if they stand up for someone else, they'll draw the Duo's attention.

Still, *I* care; therefore, I am livid and more livid.

I know I'm not supposed to hate, but I think I hate them.

I still don't mention their insults to my parents. I never have. How could I talk to them about the embarrassing things the Duo say to me? I'm afraid, if they knew, they'd take me out of school and away from my friends.

Okay, maybe there's a little more to it. I guess, on an almost subconscious level, I have another fear. What if I broke down and told them, and they didn't help me? What if they didn't believe me? What if they don't think it's a big deal, and they're indifferent like all the other adults at school?

This whole train of thought is ridiculous. I know that. My dad would be angry in the extreme. Yes, if no one else in the world would take up for me once the truth came out, he would. I can hear the slide action of the shotgun even as I begin to contemplate such an idea.

Okay, okay, I'm exaggerating about the gun . . . a little.

Anyway, can you see the crazy, disjointed paths my thoughts take?

So I continue to handle Matthew and Luke in my ineffectual way. Despite my best intentions and against all common sense, I get crazy mad and lash out with words.

It does no good.

I mean, it goes without saying: two wrongs don't make a right. I'm just playing into their plans. I guess they think it's funny when I get upset with them. Even so, I can't seem to let their comments go, at least with any consistency.

I wish they would go away forever.

Thankfully, time stops for no man—or for two evil guys—and the school week rolls to a close.

And regardless of my bumpy week, I'm looking forward to the weekend with anticipation. Our whole group is going to the Wynnewood Theater to see *Reds*.

Jack's wanted to see it since before it was released in December, so in deference to his recent heroics, we've agreed to make a night of it.

Actually, I plan on paying for his ticket. He deserves it.

When Saturday evening rolls around, we file into a row and take our seats. George is on one side of me; Charlotte's on the other.

Like a small child, George decides it's a good time to bother and distract me by poking me in the side and lightly pulling on my hair. He's usually more mature than this. It's not long before I become frustrated, grab his hand, and squeeze it with all my might. Okay, I'm not so grown-up myself. This causes a faint yelp, but afterward he decides to leave me alone. I sigh in relief. Now, if Charlotte would get her laughter under control, I could focus on the movie.

She thinks our antics are hilarious.

"Wow. That was *long*," Charlotte comments as we file out of the theater over three hours later.

"Somebody please explain to me why he ever thought Communism was such a good idea? I'm missing something," Lauri asks.

"Idealism sucks," remarks Earley.

Teresa and Pumpkin nod, but I'm not sure what to think, so I refrain from nodding *or* commenting.

I do know the movie has left me a little depressed and confused. In truth, I'm with Lauri. After all, Communism equals Cold War equals scary.

It's disappointing. I was so looking forward to seeing Warren Beatty. I mean, the movie.

"A penny for your thoughts." George elbows me to get my attention.

"We-ell, I'm not sure I have any coherent thoughts at the moment. I guess I'm sleepy and ready to get home."

"Are you? We could go grab something to eat after dropping everyone else off."

"I don't think so tonight. Sorry." But I manage to give him a tiny, tired smile as we continue toward the car.

But he doesn't give up. On the drive home, just as we're about to reach our neighborhood, George asks again if I want to go out for a quick bite.

"Another time. So-ar-ry," I apologize again around a yawn and continue, "It's almost midnight; my parents will want me home with church and everything in the morning. I think the only reason they let me stay out so late on a Saturday night was because they knew I was with you. I'll see you Monday morning. Okay?"

"Okay, sleepyhead. See you then."

"Bye. Thanks for driving tonight," I say as I climb out the passenger-side door and slam it shut.

Once I'm to the porch, I turn around to wave good-bye. As usual, George is waiting to make sure I get inside without mishap.

I can barely keep my eyes open as I turn to stagger into the house, but the thought of his caution makes me smile another drowsy, content smile.

George makes me smile a lot. Despite the Duo, and the virtual loss of Earley's friendship, I'm having a good year.

A little while later, as I lay my head down on my cloudy-soft pillow, I say a prayer thanking God for all my friends.

Especially George.

"Dearest heavenly Father: Thank you for your precious Son, Jesus. Thank you for my family and my friends. Thank you for George, Teresa, Charlotte, Earley, Jack, Lauri, and even Annie and Pumpkin. Thank you for my warm bed. Thank you for our church . . . for my family. I pray Grandma will get better. Please forgive my sins. Please forgive me for the way I react to Matthew and Luke . . ."

Then I fall asleep.

Sunday arrives. During church, I think about George and hope he's not upset because I didn't go to eat with him last night. Then I think better of it. He's a very easygoing, understanding kind of guy, and he didn't seem mad.

Monday. I think. I hear a gentle voice calling my name and feel someone shaking me.

"Lola, wake up."

"No, Mom. I need more sleep." I'm groggy, so I roll over to ease back into slumber. It can't be time to get up for school.

"Lola, I need to tell you something. You need to . . . sit . . . up," she continues.

I'm still drowsy, but I'm somehow coherent enough to hear a catch in her voice. I finally open my eyes.

Thank goodness she hasn't turned on the light. It's got to be the middle of the night. The hallway light is on, causing her to be backlit. I can't see her face, but I can see my dad's silhouette standing in the doorway.

This is not usual.

I turn over to look at my alarm clock. It's 3 a.m. on Monday morning.

"What's going on? Is Grandma okay?" My voice is raspy.

"It's not Grandma," she responds, and with that, it begins to dawn that something unexpected and awful may have happened.

"It's not Elizabeth or Earley, is it?" Worry has begun to tinge my voice, and now I'm fully awake.

"No, honey, it's George."

"George?"

No way. Nothing bad could happen to George.

"He was in an accident last night, in his car, driving home from church."

"Well, is he in the hospital? Was he badly hurt?"

She doesn't answer right away.

When she does, it sounds like her voice is stretched tight.

"Sweetheart, Henry called not long ago. They wanted us to know, George died in the accident."

Dad flips on the light.

I squint my eyes to shield them from the too bright light; then I push myself up and swing my legs over the side of the bed to stand up.

Then stop.

I'm speechless.

I'm frozen.

This can't be right.

But now I see Mom's face. Her eyes are red and puffy; her lip is quivering. She has tear tracks tracing down it, and she's clutching a tissue.

She's not looking pretty.

Is that how grief looks?

I turn to my dad. He has one of the grimmest expressions I've ever observed on his features.

Yet I think they must be mistaken.

This isn't right.

It *can't* be right.

But I know my parents wouldn't lie to me. They would be careful not to tell me something misleading—they're not cruel. And with that realization I try to stand up, but instead I lean forward, cover my mouth with my hands, and roll off onto the floor. I think I hit my head, but I don't feel it.

I barely register the thud.

I feel scratchy red, synthetic shag carpet on my face and hands. And such *sadness*.

I hear moaning, and worried whispers, and arguing, but I can't seem to stop crying. I can't even look up.

The carpet absorbs my tears. I must've tried to pull myself off the floor because I realize I'm now on my hands and knees rocking back and forth.

I think I may be the one moaning.

Oh, God, *no*.

I hear a fabricy sliding sound.

It's my mom descending from the bed onto the floor beside me. She's trying to gather me to her by sliding her arms around my body and leaning over me, but I'm too big for her to move. I feel her shaking, hear her sobs, and feel a cold spot on my back where my pajamas are now wet with her tears.

A few heavy footsteps sound toward us, and I feel her being pulled away from me. Her cries become louder; in her distress, I manage to respond.

I look over. Dad is now on the floor as well. His arm is around my mother, and silent tears make new paths . . . draw new scars . . . down his face.

I crawl over and into my mother's embrace, and she quiets. But her arms don't hold comfort.

Not like George's.

They're too small.

With certainty and hopelessness, I know no one's arms will ever hold comfort again.

Yet I stay there, and we all cry together.

Who knows for how long.

All I know is . . . all we are is pain.

We're lack of color.

We're *nothing*.

There *is* nothing, so I pull myself up and fall back into bed, leaving their grief on the floor, taking mine along with me.

I wake to the sound of my parents' voices and the feel of a large headache.

I briefly wonder why my father's home and why I'm not at school; then realization arrives like a cloud-to-ground lightning strike.

"Mom!" I choke out. The tears start up again. I don't think I can get out of bed, but I need her.

I hear her shuffle toward my room. She has a box of Kleenex in her hands, which she deposits on my bed before answering me.

"Yes, do you need something, honey?"

"I need some aspirin. Are you sure about George? This . . . hurts. If can't be *right*," I sob.

"Oh, sweetheart. *No* . . . no, no, no. It's true, but it isn't right," she whispers as she leans down to push the hair from my face. "You do have a small bump on your forehead. I'll go get you some aspirin. I know you probably aren't hungry, but do you think you could try to eat something?"

"No."

I don't think I'll ever be able to get out of bed again, and eating is for the rest of the world.

"Dad is packing to drive to Houston. He feels like he should tell Elizabeth in person. I think he's right. He's called her advisor and hopes to get her excused from classes this week, somehow." Her voice cracks a bit around the words.

She looks lost.

At the thought of Elizabeth's possible reaction, my tears ramp up even more, but my mom doesn't comment.

I mean, what is there to say?

"I'll bring you the aspirin."

I nod through my tears.

I take my aspirin but stay in bed.

I can't get up.

I can only cry until I fall back asleep, only to wake to the same nightmare.

I quickly learn why the clichéd phrase "crying oneself to sleep" exists.

After all, I'm only able to weep and sleep.

I'm living the cliché.
I am the cliché.

Ring, ring.
Ring, ring.
"Hello." I hear Mom answer the phone in the hallway near my room; then I hear what sounds like sobbing on the other end of the line.

"Elizabeth, please calm down. Please listen." My mother sounds as if she's going to start crying again.

"Well, *damn* it! Curse Catherine for calling you! Listen! Your father and I felt it would be better for one of us to tell you in person. Daddy's on his way to see you. He's probably halfway there by now."

Her voice decrescendos to a much softer tone toward the end, but I can still hear Elizabeth wailing on the other end of the line.

Nice, Christian girls don't use that kind of language, I think.

"I know, honey. I wish I was there to hug you."

I can't take hearing anymore, so I get up and shut my door.

Over the next few days, Grace flits in and out of the house to help Mom; on and off, my friends drop by to check on me.

I don't respond at first, because I don't think I can act normal enough to visit with anyone.

Elizabeth's phone call alerted me to the fact that I can't handle other people's pain after all.

I can barely handle my own.

Earley, however, comes over on Wednesday afternoon with Grace, and Mom doesn't play gatekeeper; she leads him directly back to my room.

"Thanks," I hear him whisper, and I look up at the sound of his familiar voice.

"Earley," I croak out.

"Hey, Lowly. You're not looking too good."

"Then leave. And don't call me Lowly."

I can't care enough to moderate the meanness in my tone.

He just stands there, looks away, and sighs.

A moment later he glances back toward me and quirks an eyebrow, and I notice his eyes are bloodshot.

I start crying again because I can tell he's been sad, and I hate it, and I just made it that much worse.

"I'm sorry, Earley. I'm . . . sorry," I shake my head. I know I'm the lowest of the low.

I can't stand to look at him, at his eyes, so I put my hands over my face.

But he walks over. I feel the bed bend slightly under his weight and hear the sound of him removing his shoes. I hear and feel him lift the covers and slide his legs under the blankets. I feel pressure on my hands. He's trying to pull them from my face.

So I let him.

We sit and look at each other.

He takes his thumb and tries to wipe away my tears, then gives up.

"How are Charlotte and Teresa doing . . . and Jack?" I scratch out.

"Not good."

I nod.

Then realization hits: I'm acting like I'm the only one suffering.

But I'm not.

We've all lost him.

So I look at Earley, and even though I know he's incapable of comforting me, I think he might need a big sister about now.

I'm awkward, but I put my arms around him and pull his head toward my shoulder. He complies much easier than expected.

Yet he lays stiff and still until I start rubbing his hair; then he begins to shudder with sobs.

As tears continue to stream down my face, it's strange, but I have the urge to laugh at the irony. I didn't think I could hurt any more, but seeing his grief strikes my already broken and blue heart another hit.

How is it still beating?

I wish it would stop.

Earley falls asleep.

A little while later, I hear Elizabeth's quiet arrival.

Ten minutes go by, and she pads into my room and heads straight for the bed. She looks at me and mouths a brief "love you" before climbing in beside Earley and curling around him.

He doesn't stir.

Elizabeth's fingers beckon and flex on the hand she's laid across his shoulder. I grab them and cling tightly, an unexpected lifeline.

The situation reminds me of when we were younger and would all nap together.

I wish we were still young, because then George's little, chubby body would be napping just up the street and around the corner.

An hour or so later, Mom wakes us for dinner.

The visit from Earley is good in many respects, but the main benefit is the beginning of a new resolve.

I mean, I knew in my head I wasn't the only one suffering, but seeing his grief reminds me that I've got to get up and try to function at least a little. After all, my family and friends need me.

I need them too.

So Thursday morning, I pull myself out of bed, rickety and stiff from inactivity, and get in the shower. I try to eat a real breakfast, consisting of two pieces of toast and a big glass of milk. I don't totally succeed, but it's a good effort.

Mom uses the opportunity to wash my sheets.

Like I've said, she's a good mom.

Later, Dad lets me know the funeral will be on Saturday. The announcement causes me to start crying again.

Curse these tears, I think.

I never knew one medium-sized person could shed so many.

I don't want to talk about the funeral.

It was awful.

There were too many people.

Where did they all come from?

Pumpkin and Jack were sitting off to our right side. Pumpkin, despite her copious tears, managed to look stunning in her grief.

I may dislike her after all.

The principal of our school got up to share a few brief words about George, as if he really knew him. According to Dr. Richards, all the kids at school have been holding impromptu memorials and planting remembrances around the school building.

Well, good for them, I guess.

Oh yeah. To cap it all off, I have to return to school on Monday.

CHAPTER 18

We were fifteen and had just started our sophomore year.

"Evie, you're drunk as a skunk. You can't even walk straight. Give me your car keys now." Charlotte holds out her hand and says it in such a matter-of-fact manner, it takes the sting out of her words.

"Oh, oh, Charlotte! Did you have any of the punch? They have the besssst punch. Luke gave it to me. You shush . . . try it. Did I just say shush?" Evie singsongs, then commences to cry before continuing, "Oh, my. I'm dizzy. My parents are going to kill me, aren't they?"

"Maybe. But I think they'll be so happy to have you home safe and sound that once they think this through, you might get off light. Especially after they find out you were tricked into drinkin' it. So I'll say it again—hand over the keys. Now." Charlotte continues to extend her palm as Evie digs fruitlessly around her purse.

I grow impatient and grab the purse out of Evie's hand to retrieve the keys.

"Hey! Charlotte, I don't like . . . your friend. Tell her . . . to give me my purssh back," Evie slurs. I guess she has enough fight left to ask Charlotte to rescue her from me.

"I can't find the keys, Charlotte. She must've dropped them somewhere."

"That's okay. I'll drive her home. We'll just hope someone's at her house to let her in. Anyway, I'm not leavin' her at a party like this. Someone's sure to take advantage of her."

We stagger over to Charlotte's red VW Bug, supporting Evie lightly between us. Luckily, she's not too toasted to walk with a little assistance.

Unluckily, Evie becomes sick with scant warning about a block from her house and vomits all over the back seat of the car.

The stench is overwhelming. Evie looks traumatized. Tears gush down her cheeks as she rocks back and forth, moaning and clutching a grungy towel to her mouth that Charlotte keeps in the trunk for emergencies. All I can think about is my hatred for the Demented Duo, their unexpected appearance at this party, and that they managed to doctor the punch.

I'll never forgive them.

The bright spot is Charlotte, who has enough kindness left to make sure an inebriated, nauseous, stinky Evie is delivered safely to her door; then Charlotte explains to Evie's parents the situation after they calm themselves.

Charlotte is a saint.

Walking into school is a continuation of my ongoing daymare.

Thank goodness Charlotte picked me up this morning, so we could arrive together.

Nobody bothers us during drill team, but after first period, as we're moving between classes, people stare at us and point. They know we were friends with George.

It makes me uncomfortable, but I feel too sad and tired to pay it much attention.

Truthfully, all *I* see is George's absence. In the dusty hallways; in the stinky, crowded lunchroom; in the busy parking lot. The lack of his physical presence leaves a huge, gaping tear.

It's the father of all wounds.

And like a yawning black hole, it's crushing the sunshine.

Where's my light now?

In the cafeteria, we sit and try to eat, hardly raising our heads. Talk is nonexistent.

And for some reason, this makes me cry so hard that Charlotte and Teresa decide I need to go to the nurse's office.

My mom comes to retrieve me a little while later.

The next day I try to concentrate in class, but thoughts of George intrude.

As the week progresses, I realize I've lost all interest in drill team.

I ask my parents to check with the counseling staff to see if I can be transferred to study hall or something equally benign and anonymous, because the pointing and staring are continuing, and it's really starting to bother me.

After all, I don't think I know anyone in study hall. They won't point and whisper at and about me.

My parents ask me to wait a few weeks, but I'm wondering why. What's the point?

As I become even more aware of my surroundings, I look around to see random people walking down the hallways with red-rimmed eyes and glazed looks.

Some of them I don't know.

Maybe they're crying for a different reason.

Who am I kidding, right? But it reminds me of George's popularity and the number of potentially unfamiliar people with whom he interacted and was friendly.

I wonder why, in their sadness, they look at me.

I can't help them.

I guess my friendship with George has given me unforeseen notoriety. I guess study hall wouldn't be as anonymous an experience as I was hoping.

Over the next month, I continue to do the bare minimum, and my returned assignments tell of my lack of studiousness.

Instead of the nineties and eighties that normally grace my assignments, red, slashy eighties and seventies (and even a few sixties) start to make a bold appearance.

I'm okay with it.

My parents aren't.

They're worried. We talk about it, and I try to reassure them I'll soon be bringing the grades back up, but I become a little frustrated over their intense concern.

I mean, George is dead.

Good grades won't bring him back.

Then, one Friday afternoon toward the end of February, Charlotte is giving Earley, Teresa, and me a ride home, and Teresa invites us into her house for a quick snack.

We might as well, right?

Her parents aren't home, but Teresa pulls out a tin of chocolate chip cookies. Her mother bakes them weekly to keep on hand.

We sit down at the kitchen table with big glasses of milk and three cookies apiece. I'm surprised at the hunger generated at the sight and smell of Jane's cookies. Maybe it's a good sign, because I haven't been eating well.

"Lola, we need to talk to you," Teresa begins.

Uh-oh, I think.

This was an ambush?

"We've noticed you haven't been takin' care of yourself. Your hair's often tangled, and you seem to be wearin' the same clothes a few days in a row," Charlotte continues for her.

I don't mean to, but I reflexively put my non-cookie hand up to my overabundance of dark-brown hair before I respond.

"It doesn't look *that* bad, does it? Do I stink?" I reply through my last big bite while trying to get a sniff of my underarm.

Earley starts to cough with laughter. The result: he spews cookie and milk across the small table onto Charlotte.

"Well, who's not looking so good *now*?" I add with a laugh after deciding to swallow with more care.

Teresa and Charlotte run to the bathroom to get Charlotte decookied, leaving Earley and me alone for a few minutes.

"You laughed," he says in wonder as he wipes his face; then he graces me with his beautiful, heartbreaking, lovely smile.

It causes me to tear up for the millionth time.

"Yes, Earley. Just promise me something—promise never to die. Promise not to leave me." I know it's a futile appeal, but my heart trumps the rational, as usual.

He exhales and drops a forgotten cookie onto his plate.

"You know I can't," he replies. Then he scrubs his hands against his jeans with resolution.

"I will tell you this. I love you," he whispers.

"I know. Thank you for saying it." I look away for a moment to settle my emotions.

I know he's saying it in friendship.

Just as I thought I was all those months ago.

"Why don't you say it back?" he murmurs with a tiny smirk.

I jump up and give him a big hug. I don't even know what I'm feeling, but it's overwhelming. In my exuberance, his chair begins to topple backward, but Earley's quite grown up now and strong, so he manages to keep us upright and uninjured.

I end up landing in his lap; we continue to talk, munch, laugh. He tells me I *do* smell a bit. We cry a little more.

Teresa and Charlotte soon join us; our hug grows exponentially before it melts away, leaving us back in the chairs we originally inhabited and continuing on with our cookie consumption.

During a lull, I glance over and notice Teresa's front door is open, only the screen between us and the breeze. I pause to imagine the sounds issuing through that door to the street. Sounds to which any passerby might be overhearing. In amazement, I decide the sounds would ring of friendship and happiness in their ears.

I don't think they would hear the tears.

I guess we're moving forward.

I feel guilt at the thought, but I decide to stuff another cookie in my mouth to stifle it.

A few weeks go by, and things develop into a new p-G (post-George) routine. The sun is no longer as bright, but life is, well, livable.

My grades improve a little, and I decide to stay in drill team a while longer.

I would take all the harassment in the world if it would bring George back, but the one bright spot is the effect his death has had on the Demented Duo. They're much more subdued. I seem to be off their radar for now.

And Earley and I are closer than ever. Teresa doesn't seem to mind. I'm incredibly thankful for this, because I need Earley. I need his attention, and his laughter, and his hugs.

I've always needed him.

A little more time passes, however, and I begin catching Teresa and Charlotte deep in conversations that break off when I approach. I'm guessing it's boyfriend related, and Teresa doesn't feel comfortable sharing it with me, either because I'm practically a sister to Earley or just because Charlotte has more dating experience.

It bothers me, but I have so many other things to draw my attention that I don't fret on it for long. Yet as time carries on, Teresa seems to become more and more sullen.

"Teresa, are you okay? Are you still upset about . . . George?" I barely manage to get out his name as we're walking to trigonometry one Friday, despite it being two months since his death.

We slip through the door and slide into seats next to each other.

"Well, yes, but it's not George. I'm okay," she responds in a halting manner.

"If you need to talk about it, you know I'll listen, right?" She doesn't add more, and class is starting, so I'm forced to let it go.

Later, on the way to Charlotte's car, I happen to run into Earley. He isn't riding home with us today, so I bring it up with him.

"Earley, is everything okay with Teresa? You haven't done anything to upset her, have you? Or have I?"

"What? No, I don't think so," he replies with genuine surprise and confusion on his face. A tiny wrinkle forms between his blue, blue eyes. "Why do you ask?"

I don't know how to answer. I tell him it's nothing as we part. He's going to basketball practice; I'm going home.

I hasten toward the parking lot in the belief that I've kept Charlotte waiting long enough. But as I walk up to Charlotte's car I see her and Teresa once again in a serious discussion. I think I overhear something from Teresa that sounds like "*not* her boyfriend."

Now I'm really starting to worry.

"I guess I shouldn't be asking this, but what is going on with Teresa?" I ask as Charlotte and I pull out of the parking lot five minutes later.

"Would you like some ice cream? It's on me."

"It's a little bit cold for ice cream. Although on second thought, it does sound good. Just not the Polar Bear by Lake Cliff." I eye her with suspicion. "Don't think I don't realize you didn't answer my question. Oh! And you don't need to pay for my ice cream, but thanks for offering."

Charlotte drives us to the Polar Bear a few blocks away on Hampton. It's dingy and not the cleanest, but I've been going to this Polar Bear for ice cream since before I could walk, and I've not gotten sick yet.

We take our double dips on sugar cones and walk over to the football practice field behind the nearby elementary school, Lida Hooe, leaving Charlotte's car at the shopping center.

There's a small set of stands on one side of the bare, brown field; Charlotte and I make *clank-clankity-clanking* noises as we stomp up the silver aluminum seats to the top.

The field is in its post-football season state of abandonment. We have our pick of places to sit on the bleachers, but it's still winter and there's a bit of a breeze, so we sit closely and huddle together as we eat.

Charlotte eats through her first dip with speed; then she suddenly stops and gets a serious look on her face.

"Lola, I have to talk to you about somethin'."

Well, it's about time. I asked her first, after all. "What's going on with Teresa? She's been in a funny mood the last several days. Earley hasn't done anything to upset her, has he?"

"No, it's not Earley. Well, not entirely."

"It better not be me, because I don't think I've done a thing," I assert between small bites of my sugar cone.

Charlotte doesn't answer but continues to give me a steady look.

"What is going *on?*" I demand after a hasty swallow. My voice is starting to go up in volume. I no longer feel the cold even as the wind picks up and whips my hair across my face. With irritation, I push the strands away, but when they fly back over my eyes, I seize them with one hand and with great determination stuff them into the collar of my coat. *Take that, hair!*

But the momentary distraction hasn't veered me off course.

"Come on, Charlotte. Spit it out."

"Okay, okay. Hold your horses. I need to gather my thoughts," she says with a heavy pause. She holds out her free, glove-covered hand in a stop gesture, fingers splayed.

Finally she says, "Teresa has been a bit concerned lately. You and Earley seem a little too affectionate to her."

"Oh, that's just great! You're telling me she's jealous," I answer with derision.

"Maybe. I'm not sure, Lola, but she may have a point."

"*Wh-what?*" I sputter out.

"Just listen for a minute. Please, just listen," she implores.

I cross my arms over my chest and sit there in silent but unwilling compliance. I can't believe this is happening. I'm shaken, so I look off into the distance. In fact, this conversation has me so off-balance I don't think I can look at her, because I have a feeling she's about to drop more bombs.

Is she really doing this to me?

"I'm not sure if you're even aware of it, but you seem to have a tendency to develop relationships with boys that seem to put them in a pseudo-boyfriend roll. I know you say nothin' existed between you and George. You were *only* friends. But look how it appeared to other people. You were continually around each other; you were constantly huggin' on each other and flirtin'. Think about it—do you hug me all the time?"

As she speaks, I become more and more agitated and maybe even a little horrified, feeding my growing anger even more. Is this how everyone views me, as some sort of flirt or tease, just like the Demented Duo constantly spew at me?

No. Way.

"I know you say Earley is like a brother to you, but think about it. If he really was your brother, would you be huggin' him constantly?"

Deep inside me, the heat has gone cold.

We're done.

"If you value our friendship, you'll stop right now. I can't believe you think I would play with people's feelings like that. I can't believe you're saying this, Charlotte!" I seethe out.

"Lola, you may not even realize you're doin' it . . . "

And with that, I throw my ice cream on the ground. The birds can have it.

"You know Earley has been trying to be there for me. I'm so . . . *sad* . . . still. Charlotte, when h-he died, I wanted to *die!*"

I scream the last word. Scream it to her stunned face. Stun myself. Knock myself back to the height of my grief, to the days and minutes after George died.

No! I'm not going back to that grief ever again, so right now, anger is my friend.

I pause to catch my breath, but it doesn't take long for me to start up again.

"I can't imagine people think of me this way! I can't believe *you* think of me like that! I'm walking home. I can't talk about this anymore."

Blinded by tears, I jump down from the bleachers and begin stomping across the field in the general direction of my house.

My thoughts are roiling, but I still manage to shout over my shoulder, "Oh yeah, I almost forgot. Next time Teresa has something to say to me, tell her to do her own dirty work! And congratulations on your correct use of 'pseudo'!"

It feels so right and satisfying.

Charlotte is calling after me. Maybe following me. Maybe not. "Lola, please wait! I know you've been sad! Please! Oh, gosh! Please listen to me. Lola, *stop!* Stop, stop . . . please . . . I'm sorry . . . *please* . . ."

It's even more satisfying how her voice fades behind me as I continue walking.

Now more than ever, it's clear to me.

I'm on my own.

I feel tears slide down my cheeks and roughly wipe them away.

I never want to cry again.

I'm sick of crying.

From now on, I'm stronger than that.

I'm stronger than anything.

Charlotte drops off my books at my house later in the evening.

I don't go to the door.

I have a headache.

CHAPTER 19

We were sophomores and taking French I. Matthew chose Spanish.

Believe it or not, Luke sits by me in this class, and sometimes we talk as if he is a normal human being and not my mortal enemy, causing me to let down my guard.

"Luke, why does Matthew hate me?" I question, then cringe, realizing I've used none of my innate intelligence by daring to open up that can of worms. Unfortunately, I get the reaction I realized I was likely to get as soon as the words left my mouth. His switch flips—instead of the mildly pleasant and tolerable classmate of only moments before, he flares up as if I'd asked the most insulting question imaginable.

"Because you're a worthless slut. Why shouldn't he treat you like the tease you are? All you're good for . . ." He backhands me with his words.

Well, we won't be able to interact even seminormally from this point on. We won't interact at all other than to pass assignments back and forth, which is just fine by me. But somehow, his response wounds me; I was lulled into vulnerability, and it hurts.

The days pass.
I sit by myself in the lunchroom.

My mom picks me up from school when she's able. When she isn't, I walk home.

I throw myself into my schoolwork determined to show the world I'm just fine by myself.

From time to time, one of my former friends (Lauri, Charlotte, or Annie) will try to approach me, but I peremptorily decline to join them during lunch.

Even Teresa has tried to gain my attention a few times in a tentative, weak manner. I act as if she's not there.

I'm all right as I am, I think.

At church, I sit with Mom and Dad. They ask me why I'm not sitting with my friends, but I change the subject, and they leave it. After all, my grades have picked up. They're probably thinking they should choose their battles carefully.

I'm thinking they're right to think so.

Earley greets me when he gets the chance. I usually ignore him, but I had to give him a short explanation.

It was very short.

It went like this:

"Lola, are you trying to avoid me? Have I done something?"

"No, but we can't be friends anymore." I say it with an indifferent sigh while sweeping the hair from my face. (I no longer have patience with my hair; I'm going to get it hacked off soon.)

"What? Why?"

"Ask your *girlfriend.*" I spit it out, and with that, I walk away, potentially leaving a mess in my place.

I'm okay with that. The sooner he breaks up with the green-eyed monster, the better off he'll be. Besides—I don't have a heart anymore.

Every now and then I catch one of my ex-friends giving me a concerned look.

They better stop, or I'll give them something to truly be concerned about.

I'm still on drill team, but I find it near pointless. I don't think I'm trying out for next year's squad.

I would quit now, but I'm a little uneasy about my parents' potential reaction.

I prefer to fly under their radar at present.

It's working so far.

So for now, I'm a Bisonette. I have to participate in the spring sports pep rally, which is why I'm wearing a little purple dress with silly white ruffles on the bottom of the skirt. We even have silly little ruffles on our trunks. They look like those diaper covers babies wear, only they're purple and white.

Ridiculous.

I push through the double doors of the auditorium and pause on the landing at the top of the stairs. The other drill team members are beginning to fill up the left front section facing the stage. The athletes sit in the center section and the band sits to the right.

Thump, ump, ump.

Toting a few schoolbooks, I hear a hollow stomping noise as I walk down into the front part of our auditorium and realize it's me.

I sigh. As evidenced by the stomping, I don't want to be here. Unfortunately, it's a requirement. Although on second thought, I wonder if anyone would notice if I didn't show up.

As I'm thinking this over and noting the auditorium is only about half-full, I hear someone call my name, all loud and rude, as if it's something that belongs in a sewer struggling against a sudden, too-bright light. The name-caller's voice is coming from the section where the basketball players are sitting.

My eyes skip over Earley. I know he doesn't behave like that, but I soon find the culprit.

It's Luke. He's staring right at me, waiting for my reaction.

I take a millisecond to wonder at his behavior; this is a tiny bit unusual. Matthew's more often the one up to dish out harassment, but Matthew's only now entering through the back of the auditorium, so I know he can't be the offender.

I turn toward Luke with an indifferent stare.

"What's your problem?" My voice is flat.

"You, you b—. You're my problem. You're constantly moody. Are you on the rag, or are you missing George? I guess you're not getting any now he's dead. You know, I can help you with that."

He's not very wise, is he?

I continue to stare at him; I feel my eyebrows inch up at his audacity.

"What? You have no response? That's a surprise," he continues, adding fuel to the eternal flame of my fire.

But it's not a warm, orange, glowing bonfire.

Nope. It's not inviting. It's much, much more.

It's white hot and radioactive.

The atom is about to be *split*.

But he thinks it's over. Just as he turns to look for his next victim, I drop my heavy books on the ground with a carpet-dampening thud. It's loud enough, however, for him to hear over the increasing pre-pep rally noise, so he turns back.

"What? What now, *Lola?*" he once again vomits my name as if it's the worst curse word he's ever uttered.

I shake my head as I'm walking past my assigned section, and like a heat-seeking missile, I zero in on my target and lock in.

"No. No. *No,*" I grind out. "You're not getting away with this *anymore*—you or your *perverted* friend. I'm sick of your *sick* words and your *sick* ways. You know what really bothers me about it? You think it's funny."

My mind is racing, yet I feel in control. More than in control: I feel powerful as solutions suggest themselves to me. Solutions I've been too cowardly to see.

"Well, let's see if you think it's so funny when your parents know the full extent of your insanity. I mean, seriously, what does it say of them as parents? Actually, I'm not sure they're both your parents. I think you have to be the product of a demon on at least one side."

"Wait a minute, Lola. Don't you bring my par—" Luke, the ultimate hypocrite, protests as if he's a victim.

"Are you kidding? *I'll* bring your parents into it. They're not off limits. *My* parents aren't off limits to you, or that person's in the balcony, or Petey's, or Sam's, or Lauri's, or *anyone's!* I'll bring your parents into it, and Matthew's parents, and your nonexistent slutty, older sister. You have a cranky, old grandmother? I'll bring her into it too. You finally crossed the line when you *dared* to utter George's name."

I'm right up in his face now, close enough to burn him with my glare. "You know, I used to think you were fairly smart, but that just shot out the window. You've forgotten our fathers work together. Your dad's *told* me how much he respects mine. I'm wondering how he's going to feel once the truth comes out. Your parents may just see how sadly their plan of indifference, their plan of 'boys will be boys' has worked, because they have one of the sorriest excuses for children who has ever graced the planet. Teen Hitler would have been ashamed to be your friend," I plow out in quick and deft precision without a breath.

He scoffs and tries to turn away, but I'm not done. He's just made me angrier by backing down.

"You turn around and look at me, you slimy pile of chicken feces!" I demand.

As Luke turns to face me once again, I see Earley, in my peripheral vision, stand up and start toward me. I feel a hand on my shoulder simultaneously.

I don't know or care who's touched me, but I shrug off their touch with violence.

"*Don't touch me!*" I seethe without looking to see who's the guilty party. I'm too focused on Luke, but as if I'm in battle mode, I'm able to keep track of Matthew's movements too. He's now standing behind Luke with an angry look but is oddly silent—he either has laryngitis or is biding his time.

The auditorium, moreover, is now full. I hear several students begin to chant "fight, fight, fight," and I think it sounds like the best idea I've ever heard.

"*You.* You *sorry son of a bulbous black widow*, you scuttle over here unlike the man you're supposed to be. I think you need a good beating, and I'm about to give it to you. I may end up dead, but you're going to be sorry you *ever* messed with me."

Just as my fist is about to connect with Luke's face, Earley grabs and pulls me backward.

"No, Earley, no!" I yell, but it's to no avail.

I struggle away from him, but then someone's standing in front of me, blocking me from Luke. It's all happening so fast, but I feel myself being lifted and hoisted over a shoulder as if I weigh nothing. I realize it's not Earley, but one of his basketball teammates, Juan, who plays linebacker on our football team. (He's the only one big enough to actually deserve the term.)

The sudden change in orientation vaguely registers, but I'm so angry, all I can think about is shutting the Duo down for good, despite my now ignominious departure.

I hear clapping and shouting. "You go, Lola!" and "You tell the b—, Lola!" rings throughout the cavernous expanse as I'm carried out of the auditorium, rear in the air and stupid, damned ruffles displayed for all to see.

I don't want to hurt Juan or be dropped on my head, so I'm just about to give up the fight, but I still have enough anger left in me to look under Juan's arm to shoot the finger at the Duo with plenty of emphasis. They seem to be arguing with the principal and don't notice. But I note dozens of faces registering shock and hilarity before the doors loudly clatter closed behind me.

Juan sets me down with surprising gentleness and stares at me as if I've grown a second head. I yank my silly dress down and force my even sillier hair out of my eyes.

It's not long before Earley pushes through the door, and he looks at me with enough disappointment to fill the world.

And you know what? I know I should feel guilty.

I know I should feel in the wrong, but I *can't*.

"I'm broken," I say all loud, proud, and matter-of-fact to their silent inquiry. Yep, my little light has not been covered by a bushel, but instead, has fallen off the candle stand and been stomped on.

I think I'm the one who stomped on it.

I turn to stride toward the exit just as the drill team sponsor and vice principal rush up.

I don't respond to their pleas to stop.

I don't bother to walk by my locker.

I just walk on home.

And to be frank, I'm feeling pretty good. I walked into that auditorium at about five foot five, but I walked out well over six feet.

Mom and Dad inform me I've been cut from the drill team later that evening—something to do with the use of bad language (can't they even get that right? It was an obscene gesture) and trying to start a fight.

I'm grounded for the next two weeks, but it was worth it.

Because after I and a few other people, including Matthew's girlfriend, are forced to spill about five and a half years of beans on them, Matthew's and Luke's parents decide to get involved for once. You got it: the Demented Duo and the Dreaded Dodge, Matthew's decrepit old car, are out of action—at least for a month.

Luke's parents didn't seem to know a thing. They're in supposed shock.

Matthew's parents suspected the drinking and sleeping around, as if those were acceptable behaviors, but none of them knew about the harassment, or that Matthew had been hitting his girlfriend.

I think I like being angry.

CHAPTER 20

I'm back at school the next Monday and walking the halls as if I own the place, and to be frank, I'm pretty much deemed a hero.

It feels good.

I may be grounded, but I've almost single-handedly sterilized some revolting vermin.

Somebody had to do it.

You've got it—the anger feels great, and it's useful as well. Now I no longer care what other people think of me. I'm free to set right whatever I see wrong, so I do. Some feelings may get hurt in the process, but I think we should all be looking at the big picture: a few temporarily ruffled feathers versus straightening out someone else's life for good.

It's perfect.

Not only that, but I've got a plan for the Duo when their harassment starts back up again, as I know it will. In fact, I don't care what they say or how gross it is, because I'm no longer embarrassed. I'm past it. When it resumes, I'll write down details and report them back to my dad or whoever is closest to make sure Matthew's and Luke's parents hear about it. If they don't like hearing the disgusting reports concerning their spawn, well, I have high hopes of getting those two transferred to the newly opened

Science and Engineering Magnet by the end of the school year. Let their parents be the ones who get harassed.

My only minor worry is my parents' disappointment over the pep rally situation. After they had an emergency meeting with the vice principal and drill team sponsor late Friday, they tried to talk to me over the weekend. Dad even raised his voice a bit, though more in anger at all the crud I'd been through thanks to the Duo. But Mom persisted all Saturday and Sunday in her efforts to get me to open up about "whatever is going on with me," as she put it.

"Mom, I don't want to talk about it," I repeat for the hundredth time, then, in hypocrisy, resume, "Matthew and Luke were 'going on,' and they have been for years."

"But you've never mentioned this before. What's so different now, Lola?" she persists.

"I've just . . . I've just *had* it with them." I sigh before continuing, "I was too embarrassed to talk about it before, but I can't take it anymore. They've called me the b-word for the last time, at least within my hearing or without making sure someone passes the news on to their no-good parents."

"Lola!" Mom replies in a shocked voice, but Dad agrees with me and advises her that we might as well call a spade a spade at this point.

Believe it or not, my parents mentioned (threatened) something about counseling. Are they kidding? I'm not going to a shrink. If anyone needs to go and see a psychiatrist, it's Matthew and Luke.

In any case, after all was said and done, my parents decided they understood my anger and knew I didn't start the argument, blah,

blah, blah; therefore, they were going to take it relatively easy on me. My punishment of two weeks grounding seems reasonable to me.

I don't have a social life, anyway.

I'm mulling all this over as I continue to my next class, French.

Matthew isn't in this class, but Luke is; he sat next to me, but he's been moved to the front and very much center of all his classes. As I walk past his desk, he tries to give me a token dirty look, as they've done in all the classes we've shared. Frankly, I couldn't care less. The look is completely impotent.

I smile back.

They both hurt me.

But they'll *never* do it again.

We begin our conjugation of a couple of irregular verbs; then my teacher calls on me to answer a question.

"Lola, comment s'est passé votre fin de semaine?"

"Bien, Madame. J'ai fait mon devoir et j'ai passé du temps avec ma famille," I answer.

"Très bien. Et vous, Jacques?" she continues on to the next person.

Class soon dismisses, but before I exit the room I walk up to Madame to let her know her blouse is gaping. She could use the kind hint.

"I'm not sure if you're aware of it, but when you lean over the podium everyone in the class can see down your shirt." I deliver the news as nicely as possible, note her jaw drop to the stand, then turn and stride out to the hall before she has a chance to thank me. I mean, does she want half the boys in the class craning their necks to get a better look and drooling all over their desks?

As I push my way through the crowds toward my next class, I step into the restroom to run a brush through my hair and once again muse on the tragedy of our shower-like flooring, which doesn't grace the bathrooms. The rest of the school is pretty much covered in it.

The bathroom has regular ol' industrial tile.

Go figure.

I heave the heavy door open to step through and note it closes behind me with a surprisingly quiet click; then I hear muted crying from one of the stalls.

"Who's in there?" I ask without an ounce of sensitivity.

The stall door opens with a bang, and a tear-streaked, red, angry face emerges from its hideaway. It's Jill, Matthew's girlfriend. Or it might be more accurate to say ex-girlfriend.

"Oh. It's you," I state with indifference and turn back to the task at hand.

"Yeah. It's *me*," she responds in a snuffy voice.

"Why are you *crying?* You should be having a party. The witch is dead, Dorothy,"

This seems to make her cry all the harder.

"Oh, come *on*. Please tell me you're not crying because those two worthless losers are no longer allowed in your life."

"You're heartless!" she accuses.

"Probably, but if that's the best you can do, you're a lightweight. You should've never been hanging around with Matthew. And to be frank, I bet that wasn't all you were doing,"

"That's none of your business," she ekes out. She's pathetic.

"Thank goodness," I respond to no one in particular and continue to brush my hair to the accompaniment of her ongoing sniffles, which are wearing pretty thin, pretty quick.

"Listen, you've got to stop this. You've got to pull yourself together for class," I plow on, turn the corner, and (all for free) diligently continue with the next row. "You should be thinking along the lines of 'good riddance' and giving your hands a thorough wash in preparation for the rest of your life."

Seriously, she needs help. She needs a reality check.

"You don't understand, Lola," she answers, the epitome of petulance.

Now I've lost all patience.

"No, I don't! I bet he hasn't called you or even acknowledged your presence since you finally told the truth about him. Be glad you're free of him. It's probably the best thing to ever happen to you. Be glad you're not pregnant!"

I'm ruthless, but with the last sentence she seems to cry all the harder.

That stops me for a minute.

"Oh no, no, no. Please tell me you're not pregnant with that crazy person's child."

She pauses to look at me with wide eyes and gives a few miniscule shakes of her head, her chin trembling all the while.

Whew. The relief I feel at that denial rushes out in a final sweep of vehemence.

"You've *got* to get it together! You've *got* to stop this pity party! I don't want to know any details, but you've got to realize you're better than being in a relationship with that soul-sucker. I mean, dig up some pride!" I don't get it. Can't she see that she's a thousand times better off without those two in her life?

But my words must be more than she can stand, because the next thing I know she lets out an exasperated squeal, turns on her heel, and heads out of the bathroom quicker than a comet across the night sky.

"Huh," I say to myself.

I tuck my brush back into my clutch. I'm glad I'm not her, I think, as I exit our yucky feminine haven.

When I emerge, I see Pumpkin walking down the hall looking behind her in the direction I'm guessing Jill has flown.

She turns around in time to see me. Her brow is furrowed in worry, and one perfect eyebrow rises in silent inquiry.

"I don't know anything about it," I lie, with a shrug thrown in for good measure.

I'm the picture of innocence.

Pumpkin shouldn't worry her pretty little head, after all.

Later in the week, I'm not feeling so pumped. I'm starting to miss my, um, *friends*. Maybe I'm not so okay on my own.

I begin to watch them more. Teresa and Earley are still a couple. I'm not sure how I feel about this, but they're holding hands and sitting next to each other. Yet they're not as openly affectionate as they used to be (thank goodness!), and they eat in silence.

Charlotte and Lauri stick together, whispering back and forth.

Pumpkin and Jack are discussing something. They both seem upset. He's gesturing with his hands and shaking his head. She has a surprising stubborn set to her super beautiful mouth.

Annie and Jeff continue in their own secret place. There's only ever been room for two with them, so they don't seem as affected by the changes in the group's dynamics.

So I watch and think and wonder and come to a conclusion.

The group is still sitting together, but they no longer seem united. It's as if a good marriage has fallen apart. The bride and groom no longer connect, they coexist. Not so much a tragedy as a phase, I think—but maybe it becomes a tragedy if they're stuck in the phase for too long.

Yes, I let down my armor long enough to think on these things.

Tears of frustration form at the corners of my eyes, and it disturbs me that I continue to care. So I remind myself that I don't cry while hastily wiping the unwanted drops with my crinkled-up lunch napkin. A tight ball of pain stings my chest.

I force myself to look away from them and instead focus on my faded-aqua fiberglass lunch tray. It's mellowed to a pretty color.

I give a huff of exasperation over my futile efforts at distraction and tell myself I have no more time to be weak.

I have no one left for whom to be weak.

My mouth sets in a firm and unhappy line. It's starting to feel natural, this line. I'm not sure if that's good or bad, but at least it's not turned down in grief.

I stand up, throw my clutch under my arm, and grab my tray, feeling old and stiff. I ease my chair under the table with my foot.

I start toward the exit, where I'll drop off the remains of my lunch.

If only I could dump these needy feelings for my past friendships at the same time.

If only.

For now, I'm going outside to soak up some sunshine. I want to sear my eyes with the sun and sear the thoughts from my mind.

I want to be warm for once.

But I haven't prayed in a while.

Later in the week, I'm breathing a sigh of relief. It's the end of the school day, and I can smell the freedom located just on the other side of another purple-painted door. Before I can get to the handle to reach out and grab that freedom with both hands, however, I feel someone's fingers lightly tap me on the shoulder.

It startles me, and I give a little jump.

No one's touched me in a while.

I turn to see Pumpkin looking adorably shy.

She looks a little scared as well.

I don't have time for this.

"Hey, Lola," she greets me.

"Bye, Pumpkin. Have a nice evening," I spit out before swiveling back toward the door.

"Lola! Wait!" her musical voice calls.

I give an impatient huff that's more than audible and slowly turn back around to find she's stepped back to give me more space. Smart of her, but I still don't want to talk.

I try to restrain my irritation, but it's already burst its bounds; it won't be easily subdued.

"What's up?" I respond with no grace as she, ever graceful, glides back up a few steps to my point of near escape.

"I need to talk with you for a few minutes. Would you mind walking with me to one of the empty classrooms? I promise it won't take long . . . and it's important. At least, *I* think so," she implores with a soft voice.

"Ooooh-kay," I reply in a skeptical manner.

"I promise," she whispers as she gently pulls me by the arm to get me started in the right direction.

So we weave our way through the emptying hallways until we find the deserted ROTC classroom across from the snack counter, but I'm getting angrier and angrier all the while. I mean, who does she think she is, demanding I stop to talk to her when I have so many better things to do?

"Okay, Pumpkin. What's going on?" I ask as I pivot toward her and cross my arms over my chest. I once again give her a look to convey my impatience.

"Well, I wanted to talk to you a little bit. I wanted to ask you to come back to our lunch table. We're missing you. Lola, I think—"

"Whoa, whoa. Did you just say *our* lunch table?" I say.

"Well, yes. I think we need . . ."

"Wait a minute. What makes you think the table was ever *our* table to begin with?"

I'm evil. I know it. I can't help it.

"Well, we've been sitting there all year . . ." she manages to get out.

"*Listen* to me, and listen closely. I've been sitting at that table with my so-called friends since the first day of my freshman year. I'm not sure it's 'our' table. I'm not sure you're part of the '*our*' table equation. I think you're an interloper and never belonged in the first place. I never understood how you ended up there at the beginning of the year. Did anyone invite you?" I spit out the words in rapid-fire bursts. Besides, I've already had Earley stolen from me. Why do Teresa and someone like too-perfect Pumpkin continue to usurp my friendships while I sit on the outside alone?

"Yes," she murmurs.

"Who?" I command.

"Jack. He said it would be okay for us to sit with you."

"He was *wrong*," I seethe out and rocket on. "Jack was welcome, but I don't understand why you haven't been sitting with your other pretty friends over at the pretty cheerleader table. Aren't you too good for the rest of us? Don't you *really* think you belong with those who are like you, all pretty, and fake, and with a perpetually boring personality?"

Tiny tears are forming at the ends of her supernaturally long lashes; unsightly beads of sweat begin to form on her upper lip. "How can you say that? You're not acting like yourself. Please *listen*—" she pleads.

"No, Pumpkin. You've got it wrong. I'm acting *exactly* like myself. This is who I am now. I once thought there might be a happily ever after, but now I know it only exists for pretty princesses like you. Go back to your ivory tower. Leave my friends alone. You're too good to sit at their ugly, ordinary lunch table. Actually, I bet if you asked the lunchroom staff, they would pull out a gold-plated tray just for you. It would probably have a few daisy petals scattered around it."

I spit it out with enough venom to kill the world.

I think it should, at the least, kill her hope of doing me any good as I spin around and stomp toward the exit to the sound of her ladylike crying. Besides, even with the tears, her light shines too brightly. It hurts my eyes.

"Don't cry too long. It will make your face all red and puffy," I say saccharine-sweet as I walk out the door.

What's wrong with her?

Can't she see I'm a lost cause?

George, *why* did you die?

But I don't want to think about George.

I don't want to think about George ever again.

CHAPTER 21

A few days pass.

It's been quiet.

I feel oddly tired. I've been sleeping a lot.

Has all this anger, my only friend, drained me of energy?

It's Wednesday night; I've agreed to attend church with my parents. Calvary hosts a communal meal on this evening as well as a worship service.

I'm not happy about going. I haven't attended on Wednesday for several weeks. But I want to stay on my parents' good side. And let's face it, I've been grounded, and as much as I was relieved at the punishment, I'm now dying to go anywhere other than home and school.

We enter the lower floor, a sort of half-basement with a kitchen to one side, to a very familiar setup: rows and rows of paper-covered tables, the smell of chicken-fried steak, and the sight of iced tea soldiers lined up in rows, with the sweetened separated from the unsweetened, of course.

Come to think of it, I've been missing church mashed potatoes and rolls. I've been eating those mashed potatoes and rolls every Wednesday night since I was able to handle semisolid food. Now that I'm within smell of them, I wonder if I may be going through withdrawal.

My parents and I get in the line. My dad pays; the lady manning the trays, silverware, and money hands us little orange tickets for our meal.

Dad passes mine down to me as I grab my tray; we say thank you and move forward.

"How are you tonight, Lola? I haven't seen you in a while," inquires Mrs. Barrett, one of the sweet ladies who volunteer to serve us each week.

"I'm fine, Mrs. Barrett. Thanks for asking." I manage to sound polite. It must be the hunger.

"I bet you would like some extra mashed potatoes tonight."

"Yes, please. Thank you," I answer with amazing genuine gratitude and anticipation considering my ongoing attitude.

We finish picking up our drinks and head toward a table. But just as I set my tray down and reach to pull out my chair, I feel a peremptory—almost sharp—tap on my shoulder.

I turn to find Jack standing behind me. He looks as if he's vibrating with energy.

Just the opposite of how I feel.

"I need to talk to you," he says without preamble.

"Can it wait? I'm about to eat," I say as I nod at the oh-so-obvious evidence to this fact behind me.

"No. It's important. It can't wait. We need to talk *now*."

His tone's starting to make me nervous, because he sounds as if he's on the edge of losing it. I certainly don't want that to happen around my parents. I'm still trying to avoid tripping their wires, and if Jack lets any of my school behavior slip, they may start talking about a shrink again.

"Sure. Mom, Dad, I'll be back soon."

"You need to *eat*," Mom responds with a look sharper than the tines on her fork.

"I will. I bet this won't take long. Right, Jack?"

"Right. It won't take long at all," he clips.

I grab the roll off my plate and reluctantly follow him out of the lower floor, but he doesn't stop right away. He heads up a stairwell that leads to the dark sanctuary and then takes a passageway that connects to the educational building. Once inside, he opens a rarely used door. Inside is another stairwell dusty from disuse; this one leads to the roof.

Teresa and I have been up this set of steps many times during our explorations of the church.

Yet he doesn't stop on the stuffy landing but stomps up the stairs, scattering dust bunnies, and opens the door to the outside.

I'm tired and not at my best, but his earlier sharp demands and the stomping reinforce my opinion that he's not in a good mood.

I follow him out and stop just outside the roof door. I let it go too soon, and it closes behind me with a loud bang; a few birds nesting at the other side of the roof squawk and flap their wings in protest.

I turn back from the noise to see Jack pacing back and forth, back and forth, back and forth. Roof gravel scatters and skitters at his feet as if trying to get away from him. I'm guessing the energy rolling off him could power about half the city.

I think I'll let him start the conversation.

So I wait . . . and I watch him pace . . . and the tension grows.

"I don't want to do this, but I have no choice," he mumbles more to himself than to me. "No one else . . ."

Then he takes a deep breath and turns to face me.

I let out a tiny, involuntary gasp because there's a look of *mission* in his eyes. It's overlaid with what I'm afraid may be quite a bit of anger. I've never seen Jack angry before; I hope I'm misreading him.

I'm not.

"I've *had* it with you!" He's not shouting, but he walks closer. His stare pins me like a bug to corkboard, making me uncomfortable to an unmentionable degree.

I look off to the side. "What?" I disingenuously respond.

"Look at me. You heard me. I'm not repeating it."

I swivel my eyes back toward his face to find he's moved even closer. I inch back toward the door.

"Well," I say, my eyes traveling once again, "could you be more specific?"

"ARE YOU *KIDDING* ME?!" he roars, blowing out the speakers.

I drop my roll; the birds nesting at the other end of the roof decide it's finally time to take flight.

"You *know* what I'm talking about, but just in case you've forgotten, let me refresh your fragile memory. *Pumpkin* is what I'm talking about. *Jill* is what I'm talking about. The Duo. And Charlotte, Teresa, and Earley!"

"I don't think that's any of your business, Jack," I bluster while crossing my arms over my chest. My heart feels like it wants to pound right out of me. Anger and pain and confusion and maybe even something like shame all thudding out like a wrecking ball in my ribcage. How does he know about Jill, anyway? Are there no secrets?

"I don't care if it's 'any of my business'!" he says while using finger quotes, "I'm making it my business! I'm tired of seeing the path of destruction Hurricane Lola is leaving in her wake!"

Tears prick my eyes; I hate them. I don't cry. I don't want to cry ever again. "That's not fair, Jack! You don't understand. Charlotte and Teresa insulted me. And the Duo . . . Matthew and Luke . . . how can you take up for them?" I answer in agitation. "I did everybody a favor confronting them!" And that powerful anger feels so much better than all the paralyzing pain.

"No, you listen to me. You're the one who doesn't get it. I don't know what's going on between you, Teresa, and Earley, and I don't want to know, but the day you hurt Pumpkin was the day your days as the school bully were numbered!"

For a minute I can't breathe right.

"School bully? How can you say that?"

He glares at me. "You're not getting me off track. Deep down, you *know* what you've been doing. But Pumpkin . . . how could you say those things to *Pumpkin?*"

I start to answer, but he cuts me off.

"You stand there and listen up. I need to tell you a story." He stops for a nanosecond, then barrels on. "Last year when she became cheerleading captain, a few members of the squad decided they weren't happy about it. They started harassing her late last spring. They vandalized her house and her car, they and their friends. They would shoe-polish the word 'slut' or worse on anything of hers they could get their hands on. Then turn around and call her frigid because her parents don't allow her to date."

Those stupid tears are back. No, *please*. "I don't see what this has to do with me; I don't want to hear anymore." I turn to leave but realize I've backed all the way into the door; he's got me so hemmed in, I don't have enough room to turn around to pull it open.

"YOU'LL STAND THERE AND LISTEN!" he thunders, finger pointed at my face.

I bend in on myself. Recross my arms over my chest . . . to protect my heart. I've never before wished that I couldn't hear, until now.

"George and I found her *cornered* in between the buildings by four strange guys not long before school let out for the summer. They were *pushing* her and calling her names. They were making suggestions so disgusting the Duo would've been offended. If we hadn't walked up, I'm not sure what would've happened. I'm sure you'll believe it when I say we think some of the other cheerleaders may have been behind it."

The world is crashing in.

I don't want it to come down on me.

I can see Pumpkin's stricken expression when I lashed out at her.

And George.

"*No* . . . I don't want to hear this . . . don't talk about George," I plead.

"Why do you think she hangs around me all the time? Why do you think we decided to sit with a tableful of juniors and a sophomore during our senior year of high school? Were you too full of yourself to stop and *think?* Lola, George and I were the only two people she felt safe with. She couldn't sit with George at lunch. He was continuing to date Michelle even though he knew some of her friends might've been in on Pumpkin's harassment. Besides— do you think *Michelle* would've put up with Pumpkin hanging around George for protection? C'mon!"

He steps back and starts pacing again. He's no longer looking me in the eye; even so, I'm pretty sure he has more to say.

But as he's pacing, he quiets. It's quick, but I know he's not finished; his fists are clenched; his focus isn't diminished.

He says it in a forceful whisper. "Lola, I told her she would be safe with you. With *us.* I told her you were kind and so were your friends. I promised her she would be welcome."

I can't take it anymore. I walk away from the door . . . from him . . . to the parapet at the edge of the roof. I don't want to hear another word.

I feel those stupid tears slide down my cheeks once again and lean my forehead down on the cool metal edging the bricks.

"Please stop, Jack. *Please* stop," I murmur.

But he's followed me.

I feel his hand between my shoulder blades. I want to cringe away, but I'm too weak to move.

"What would George think, Lola? He said you were one of the most important people in the world to him. What would he think?"

"No. Please don't talk about George, Jack. I'm sorry. I'm so, so *sorry*, but don't talk about George."

I hear his feet crunch on the gravel as his footsteps fade toward the door.

"I used to think you were one of the best people I knew, Lola . . . you and George. I thought you were safe. You may be sorry, but I'm not sure I'll ever be able to forgive you for what you've done to Pumpkin."

I hear the door clatter shut behind him.

I hear the door clatter shut on my sobs.

I turn around and slowly slide down the wall. My shirt catches on the prickly brick and the back rides up.

The bricks are etching cruel lines into my back as George's death etched cruel lines into my heart.

And I cry as if I've lost George all over again.

I cry about the cruelty of this world.

"Why, God, *why?*" I whisper and with that tiny prayer realize where my anger has been directed all along.

"WHY, GOD? WHY? *WHY* DID HE HAVE TO LEAVE ME? *WHY* DID YOU TAKE HIM FROM ME?" I scream at the stars.

I hack out my prayer between sobs. "I can't *stand* it. Why is my life full of *nothing?* Just kill me. I don't have the guts to jump off the roof, but you could send a big wind . . . and it would pick me up and pull me toward the sky . . . and then drop me. Then I could be with him again . . . and I wouldn't be so sad."

I crouch there and wish to fly like a bird, instinct on wing, to quickly drop from the sky.

And all the pain would end.

Please, God. Please forgive me, but I can't take this anymore.

Earley finds me a little later. I'm lying on the roof, but he pulls me up and helps me down the stairs. He even goes into the ladies room with me to help me wash my face and get the gravel out of my hair.

I guess it's okay, because everyone else is in the service.

He makes me eat a candy bar that he's stashed in his pocket. It has no taste, but I comply.

I think he says something about Jack pulling him out of the lower floor and telling him I needed some help. And where I was.

Earley is God's angel, I think. I bet Earley can fly.

And I bet Earley wouldn't fall.

CHAPTER 22

I'm still tired. I walk like a zombie through the rest of the week. I try to block out Jack's words and not think of what I've done.

It works for a few days, but his words are persistent. They won't let me be.

They cause me ever-escalating discomfort. They work to grow these increasingly painful twinges of regret.

I *fight* to stay unfeeling. I continue to rationalize my actions, but his accusations are relentless; they sink in deeper and deeper. It's as if each word has been drawn into my memory with a fine sharp point that is growing into the strokes of a thick, ugly, black permanent marker.

My memory is normally not this airtight, but *his* words are not going *anywhere*.

I have perfect recall of each and every one.

The little pings of embarrassment then start. They quickly grow into huge gongs of shame.

I *hate* shame.

Normally, when I feel shame or embarrassment I end up getting angry with the culprit, but I can't bring myself to be angry with Jack. Before last Wednesday, he was always kind to me.

Which begs the question: Was he truly *un*kind last Wednesday?

I'm not sure.

Maybe *I'm* the culprit.

I cringe.

These thoughts are wearing on me, emotionally and physically. I'm getting by. That's all.

It's been a little over a week since the night Jack confronted me. I'm trudging home, trailing my book bag along behind me on the sidewalk. Periodically, it gets caught on rough spots in the patchy, gray path; I have to stop and untangle it.

The walk home isn't far, but when my bag gets tangled once again, I leave it and sit down on the curb near the corner of Marvin and Plymouth. I fold my arms across my knees and lower my head to their protection.

I'll get up in a minute, I tell myself. I'm almost home.

I hear a car drive up. Not unusual, but it stops.

I don't want to look up.

I hear its door slam and high-heeled footsteps approach.

I feel someone sit down next to me.

I'm wondering who's coming to rescue me now.

I'm wondering if anyone would *want* to rescue me now.

It must be a mistake.

"Lola. Is that you?" The voice is familiar, soothing, and soft, in close proximity to my ear.

I look over to see Grace sitting on the curb in the most ladylike manner imaginable. It's completely unlike my blue-jeans-clad sprawl.

"Grace," I whisper in surprise as if her name has deeper meaning.

She can't be real—I'd forgotten about her.

"Yes, honey. It's me. I left work a little early and saw you on the corner. Are you all right? Would you like a ride home?" she asks in kindness, concern tingeing her voice.

I have no answer, but I manage to shrug my shoulders while placing my head back onto my arms (no easy feat).

Then I begin to cry for the gajillionth time.

"Why don't you come home with me for a while? I bet your Mom isn't back from class yet. After all, we haven't been able to spend any time together lately. I'm missing my Lola. I think I need a little Lola time," she gently jokes while stroking my hair.

I raise my head with a look of hope and do the bravest thing I can possibly do: nod my head yes.

She stands up with a little wobble, smooths her skirt down, and inclines her head toward the car; then she starts in its general direction, easily untangling my book bag along the way.

I follow, sniffling.

As I get into the car, she hands me a tissue about the same time she throws me a life preserver.

"Tell me what's wrong," she demands with affection as she turns the key in the ignition.

"I'd love to," I choke out with enough sincerity to fill the world.

I dry my tears as we make the short drive.

Maybe, just maybe, Grace will be able to help me put away the tissues (and the anger) for a long, long while.

I'm thinking no one but God can help me with the grief.

A short while later, I'm sitting at their breakfast bar. It's pale blue instead of bright yellow like ours, but thin, wavy lines meander and twist around inside the color in a manner similar to our own.

The lines rivet me. I follow one with my eyes; then follow it with my finger as I drink my hot chocolate, and Grace drinks her iced tea.

Focusing on the lines seems to help me talk, so I follow them closely, trying to push dots of condensation from Grace's tea around the surface as if the drops follow a fascinating treasure map that will soon yield buried treasure.

I think the distraction helps me to remain calm.

I'm not sure.

So I start at the beginning—the beginning of the year that is.

I tell her *everything*.

And continue to follow the lines with my finger.

And Grace listens.

She's a good listener. When I'm brave enough to look up to catch her eye, she's still got her kind gaze pinned on me, but not in a way to make me squirm.

It's more in a way to let me know she cares.

She loves me.

She's on my side

So I talk.

A few hours later we're interrupted by Earley's arrival.

I stopped talking about thirty minutes ago, but Grace pulled me over to the couch; I've been lying there with my head in her lap.

She plays with my hair, braiding and unbraiding a thin strand.

But as Earley enters the room, I struggle to sit up. I need to get home, after all. We left a note on the door for Mom, but she'll soon have dinner ready.

"Hi," Earley greets us as nonchalantly as if I held the permanent fixture status I formally boasted in their household, before he started dating Teresa.

"Hey," I respond, eyes glued to the carpet.

I shuffle to the door. Grace walks me out, then walks me toward the street.

We hear a small noise behind us and realize Earley's followed us to the threshold. He stands, a darker shadow, just within the opening. So Grace continues on up the block with me until we're enveloped beneath the boughs of the magnolia at the edge of my yard and he's out of earshot.

"Lola, I know there's far more to what's been going on, but I'm sorry Earley hurt you. You know I think he hung the moon, and I know you think he hung the moon, but he didn't really hang the moon, did he? But I also know he's going to be your friend no matter what. Eventually, you'll both need to figure out the new dynamics of your friendship, but for now, you have other things to deal with." She adds with more certainty and volume, "Listen, I've got a good idea. Why don't you come over for dinner next Wednesday night while your parents and Earley are at church? I could still use more Lola time. Okay? I'll call Eleanor to make sure it's all right with her."

I nod my head yes because I have no more words, and any I could drag up would be insufficient to express the hope she's given me. I'm too talked-out anyway.

Plus she's right about whatever I feel for Earley. It can wait. It can wait a long, long time. Maybe even forever.

I *do* have enough energy to crush my body against Grace's one last time for the night; it's good to know it won't be the last time for a long time.

It's a huge relief.

She's just what I need.

The next Wednesday, instead of going to church, I head over to Grace's. We sit and eat, and I continue to tell her all the confusing and sad details of my year.

Every now and then we laugh at the ironies, and we cry at the tragedy. And I continue to visit her every Wednesday for the next couple of months, but in the meantime (and fairly quickly), we come to some conclusions.

The only way to even begin to clean up my mess is by admitting my missteps to God and to the other people I've hurt.

The admitting them to God part, that's pretty easy. He's promised to love me no matter the debacle. But admitting them to others . . . I'm not sure I have enough courage.

So we sit on the couch and talk and pray, and I ask God for forgiveness, and I even have the audacity to ask him for a little wisdom. Because I guess I have to admit I may not be as smart as I thought I was.

And I ask him for an ocean full of bravery, because that's what it will take.

Then Grace and I discuss strategy.

CHAPTER 23

It's been a couple of weeks since our first Wednesday night, and we've decided it's time to start Operation Reconciliation.

I'm nervous. In fact, *nervous* is an understatement.

I'm not tired, however. I promised Grace I would start taking better care of myself. Eating better and more regularly seems to be helping my energy level and state of mind.

But I am anxious. This is a risk that could go badly, but we've talked about whom I should approach first and how I should approach them. And despite the nervousness, I don't think I can wait any longer to get this underway.

That's why I'm waiting outside the girls' gym after first period. I jogged all the way over from study hall.

I'm no longer on drill team with Charlotte, but she's about to walk out those doors.

I hover on a stairwell a little above and behind the gym exit like a vulture ready to pounce on its next victim. She won't be able to see me until after I've seen her; I don't want her to run, after all.

The girls begin to filter out of the gym, but it seems to take forever. Then I see her.

"Charlotte!" I call as I jump the last three steps to the bottom.

She stops in her tracks but doesn't turn around, so I approach with caution.

"Charlotte," I call much more softly this time and circle around to see her face.

She's looking a bit frozen, as if she's guarding her expression, but she hasn't run.

I decide that's a good sign.

"Hey. I was wondering if we could talk after school. Would you mind giving me a ride home?"

She's not looking at me. It's almost as if she's afraid. But she gives a barely perceptible nod. It's enough.

"Thank you," I whisper as I turn and jog off. I'm not sure she heard the last part.

But it doesn't matter. In fact, I don't stick around to find out.

I'm too big of a chicken.

Then the one school day I might wish to drag flies by at the speed of light.

I don't think the fastest rocket-ship-to-be could catch up with this day.

It zips.

It zooms.

It's over.

So I walk to Charlotte's car. I try to walk slowly, but it's as if the world is one big, super-fast slide, or I'm a magnet, and Charlotte's red VW is my opposite. It's pulling me along without any effort and despite my efforts to slow myself down.

I'm there.

And there stand Charlotte *and* Earley.

But Charlotte doesn't just stand and wait. She starts walking toward me; then she runs.

And the next thing you know she's hugging me with all her might and saying *she's* sorry over and over.

And she's crying.

I didn't expect that.

Not at all.

I'm equipped for crying, though, so I pull out a tissue and help to dry her tears; then I ask her why in the world is she saying she's sorry when I'm the biggest loser in the world and would she please forgive me.

She can't seem to talk, but she lets out a teary laugh and nods her head yes; then we walk toward her car where Earley is waiting.

All the better, I think. I can kill two birds with one stone.

Objective One: Reforge Friendships is underway.

A little while later, we're at my house pillaging my cabinets for a snack, just like we should've been all along.

I pull out a box of Pop Tarts, and we divvy up the contents.

Earley helps himself to the milk in the fridge and pours each of us a glass. I don't have to remind him where the glasses reside, thank goodness. It's only been a month or so since my argument with Charlotte, so he hasn't forgotten a thing.

We sit cross-legged on the rug in front of our fireplace with our tart-filled plates in our laps.

And they talk about their day.

They're happy.

I indulge in the luxury of their banter for a while.

It's wonderful.

But I know I have more to do.

"Charlotte?" I interrupt.

"Hmm?" she manages through a mouth full of artificial strawberry filling.

"I think I need to take some responsibility for what happened between us. I mean, thank you for saying you're sorry, but I have to apologize for stomping off the way I did. Even if I didn't agree with everything you were saying—or maybe I wasn't ready to hear it; I don't know—but I should've stayed and listened, and not been so defensive. Your friendship means too much to me to throw it away in a fit of anger." I get the speech out with precision, just as I practiced.

She looks at me with wide eyes and manages to swallow, then gives her silky, blonde head a little shake as if she's clearing it.

"Wow. Lola, I can't believe you said that, but I was wrong. I thought I was doin' the right thing. I had good intentions, but I needed to stay out of it. I think we should let it go. I think we should forget about it."

With that last statement, I feel Charlotte has almost certainly gained back her legendary tact and wisdom.

Seriously, what could be better than a friend who not only forgives but also forgets?

Very little, I think to myself.

There's more to say, however.

"Earley, I'm sorry for cutting off our friendship. I'm especially sorry for the way I did it. Can you forgive me?"

"Oh, please. A little temper tantrum is nothing new to me," he teases. "As far as I was concerned, it was never an issue. Now you *did* elbow me in the gut during that whole pep rally disaster. You probably should apologize for that, Lowly."

"Never!" I shout in my happiness.

His silliness is so contagious I decide I need to throw a bit of Pop Tart at him, which he tolerates really well. Then I give Charlotte a high five, almost upending our plates in the process.

So we finish our snacks, continue to talk, and kid each other.

"Robin asked me out," Charlotte interjects with a blush.

"Wow. Really? *Cool!*" I respond while Earley groans in the background.

"No talk of love lives," he dictates while waving around his last remaining crust. For some reason, he never finishes the edges.

Charlotte berates him for his dictatorial declaration, but his comment reminds me we're not complete.

We've got D'Artagnan and two of the Musketeers; one of the Musketeers is missing.

Of course, it may not be super obvious to my two companions. Teresa didn't usually hang out at my house after school like the other two.

But on second thought, I decide they know. They're letting it go. For now.

It's not long before Mom arrives home, and the huge smile on her face at the sight of my two friends belies how quiet she's been about their absence.

She's been worried.

So I give her a kiss on the cheek for no good reason as we walk them out the door.

"See you tomorrow!" I shout after them.

"See ya, Lola!" they respond.

"Love you, guys," I add under my breath.

I'm happier than I can contain.

The smile on my face is as big as Texas.

"Dearest heavenly Father, thank you, and please help me with the rest because I can't do this on my own," I pray that night as I close my eyes for sleep.

I approach her before church the next Sunday night.

"Teresa, can we talk?"

Youth choir has just let out, and I've caught her in the hallway before she walks to the youth center for Sunday night Bible study.

"Sure," she says. Unlike my mom's over-the-top smile of a few days ago, her voice is sure and steady; it doesn't hint at any underlying emotion. "Where?"

"Maybe we could sit outside on the steps somewhere. It's . . . nice out tonight." I sound awkward, but there's no help for it.

She nods in agreement but doesn't make eye contact with me as she heads out the nearby door.

I follow.

We don't talk as we walk, nor do we walk side by side. In fact, she walks as if she's walking to her own execution. Her back is too straight, and her stride is slightly too slow.

We proceed down a short, paved path and then turn right. Instead of crossing the street to the youth center, we continue walking, make another right, and climb some steps that lead to the sanctuary. They're at the front of the church and face W. Tenth St.

She leads, and I follow. She leads all the way to the top of the stairs where she turns and primly perches on the top step, her hazel gaze pinned straight ahead. She's not relaxed.

At all.

But I drop down next to her, and even though I'm not sure where to begin, I launch the conversation.

"Teresa, I'm not sure how to say this, but I'm sorry—"

But just as I begin my apology, she tilts her head up to the heavens, closes her eyes, and holds up one little hand in a stop motion.

"What?" I'm confused by her interruption.

"Wait, Lola, wait. I need a minute to think about this. Okay?"

Her reaction is a mystery; her face is scrunched up in concentration, and she releases a pent-up, quiet breath.

"Okay." I'm worried about what she might say. Will she even hear me out?

Time slows to turtle speed as we sit there. I'm pretty sure only a minute or two have passed, but it feels like a millennium.

She finally breathes out an even bigger sigh, opens her eyes, and begins to speak.

"Before you go any further, I want to let you know I'm sorry too. It was unintentional. I didn't mean to, but I know I egged Charlotte on. This is hard for me to admit, but . . . Lola, I like Earley a lot. I have for a *long* time, despite the fact you've always been so close to him, which should've been a big no-no to my feelings. Truthfully, before I started dating him, maybe even after I started dating him—okay, okay, I need to be honest, definitely *after* we started dating—I've been jealous of his relationship with you. In fact, I'm pretty sure Earley sensed my insecurity."

That certainly clarifies some of her out-of-character behavior at the beginning of the school year. And maybe his too. Not that I hadn't suspected. Now it's my turn to sit and think, because it was for no good reason that she's been keeping things from me for so long.

"Okay, I accept your apology. Thank you for being honest. I guess it's not a well-kept secret that your girlfriend status has been tough for me. Not because I felt Earley and I should be dating, but because he's one of my best friends. Before you started dating, I considered him my best friend. So it was pretty difficult for me when he cut me off like he did."

"Yeah. I didn't tell him to do that, by the way," she interrupts.

"I know, but I would like to say, I'm sorry for not talking this out with you sooner. Teresa, I hope from now on that you'll trust me enough to know I would never do anything to intentionally hurt whatever you have going on with him. And maybe you and Charlotte are right. Maybe I am more affectionate with him than I should be. I'm not sure, but if you want me to be more careful about it, I'll try." I swallow hard and carry on, "I want *you* to be more straightforward with me."

She must like what she hears, because she nods her head and smiles her sweet, small smile in response.

It's been too, too long since I've seen it, that smile.

So I look at her face and cherish every soft freckle.

And her honesty and forgiveness tightens up my barely-beating heart. It heals it just a little more. So even though I know she doesn't like to hug, I scoot over close to her and lean my head on her shoulder.

"I love you, Teresa. I want us to be friends forever."

"I love you too." She puts her arm around my back and pats my arm.

I know our relationship isn't fully healed. I know it's probably going to take more time, but we're okay for now.

And time can be miraculous.

So we continue to sit on the steps looking out over the street.

Navy blue encases us.

Streetlights blink on and cars swish by; home lights beckon. We talk, we pray, and I try not to think of another dusk spent on a park bench not so long ago.

We'll never fully discuss her relationship with Earley.

Or my true feelings for him.

It's going to be a bit tricky at times and maybe a bit prickly, but I'm okay with that.

Sometimes friends need barriers. Sometimes we need boundaries.

We don't have to know every thought and every experience to love each other.

We just need to know when to cross the barrier and when to stay put.

The next few weeks pass.

At lunch, I'm still not sitting at my old table.

I would brave it, but the continued glares from Jack are a bright, flashing marquee with the words STAY OUT! broadcast for me alone.

Charlotte, however, is temporarily joining me at midday, a huge comfort. Once this is cleared up, we'll all sit together again.

Until then, it's good to know I have the armor of my friendships with her, Teresa, and Earley.

So I bide my time and hope for an opening.

In the meantime, I try to find Jill for Objective Two: Conquer the Jill, but every time I catch a glimpse of her in the hallway, it's not the time or the place to approach her. Even more so than with Charlotte, and with good reason, I'm afraid she'll run as soon as she sees me in the vicinity.

In fact, I think I've seen her scurry away a few times when I've come close to her general neighborhood. As she hurries off, her friends' quizzical looks confirm my suspicions *and* indicate she must not have broadcast our encounter.

That in itself is a bit worrying.

But I get an unexpected chance at last.

One day after school, I stay late to help Mr. Atwood paint some props for the upcoming musical, my only contribution this year.

"Lola. You're using the wrong paint color. The stage lights will wash out the pale yellow paint. Those flowers should be *red*. Tsk, tsk. I saw you roll your eyes, young lady," the Monarch of the Choir Room dictates with a twinkle of amusement in his eye and strides off before I can ask him to what red paint he's referring.

There's no red paint in sight.

I sigh.

After all the mistakes I've made, I try not to get defensive, but it's difficult.

Usually, the best I can manage is to stay quiet. If only I would stop making the faces.

So I push myself up from my position kneeling over the large, wood-framed canvas covering the floor and decide to check his office for more paint.

As I walk out of the choir room, I spy a familiar figure emerge from another classroom down the hall.

"Jill!"

I guess it's no surprise that I startle her with my spontaneous shout; she literally jumps about a foot in the air.

This makes me want to snicker, but I stifle it. I'm thinking laughter won't win me any points with her.

"Jill! Wait, *please*. I need to talk to you," I beg as I hurry down the hallway toward her.

Despite my declaration, she starts to walk off.

Then she pauses.

Her obvious apprehension around me is painful to see. In profile, she fidgets with her purse strap and bites her lip; but then she straightens up, turns to face me, and shows a little backbone.

"Lola, don't come any closer if you're going to be mean to me again," she insists in the firmest voice I've ever heard her use.

"Oh! No. I promise. I promise to be nice. Okay?"

"O-kaaaay," she responds, a heavy dose of skepticism in her tone, but I see her exhale, and her mouth relaxes a fraction.

"Can we talk for a minute? Although I'm not sure where," I ask in the most confusing manner possible.

"How about we go back to the choir room? Didn't you just come from there?" she suggests with a touch of sarcasm.

"You know what? That's a *really* good idea. Thanks!" I ignore her tone of voice and throw in a reassuring smile for good measure.

The smile must work a little, because I glance over and notice her mouth easing even further as we retrace my path.

Unfortunately, when we walk in, Mr. Atwood is patrolling the room again.

"Lola, why didn't you tell me you didn't have any red paint? Oh. Hello, Jill. I'm glad you're here. You can show Lola how this stuff is supposed to be done. She's not a real artist like *you*," he says as he places the red paint down on the floor by the canvas.

I look at Jill in surprise, and she blushes.

"I take art classes," she informs me with a shrug as Mr. Atwood breezes out of the room once more.

"Wow. That's neat. I had no idea," I answer in the most unoriginal manner possible.

"No, you wouldn't, would you? You don't know me well," she emphasizes while looking me right in the eye.

I pause.

Of course she's right.

"Let's forget about the scenery for a minute," I say. "Would you mind sitting down with me so we can talk?"

She hastily shrugs off her backpack and throws it on a chair along with her purse.

"No, I won't sit down with you, but we can talk as we work on this scenery together. You know, these flowers shouldn't be pale yellow. They won't show up. Hmmm. I'm wondering what kind of color we'll get by adding the red over the yellow. It's dry, so not a true orange." And she's off working on my job.

I stand there a minute in amazement, nod my head, and ask her for guidance as, with hasty movements, she begins to sketch in more greenery around the park bench surrounded by flowers.

"You finish going over the yellow flowers with the red paint; then we'll dig out the brown for the bench. I'll probably handle that myself. I may want you to start on the green."

So we paint.

And other than the occasional direction she gives me, we stay pretty quiet. But I watch her work out of the corner of my eye.

I'm in awe.

She's taken a simple scene—a simple, everyday, one-dimensional scene—and almost (*almost*) brought it to life.

I watch her. I watch her dance around the paper. I watch her draw and paint and shade. I watch her add some camouflaged green faces peeking out from under the bench amid the flower stems and a scowling garden gnome, bearing a close resemblance to Matthew, far back under a tree.

I watch her add incredible value to something that just a little while ago was practically worthless.

And I try to help.

I get in the way, but I *try*.

So I watch our hands get dirty, and I feel my knees begin to ache, but I don't care.

It's peaceful.

Creating is peaceful.

"What do you think?" Jill queries with a content smile.

"I think it's wonderful, and I think you have wonderful talent," I matter-of-factly reply.

She looks up.

"Thanks," she murmurs back in a scratchy voice.

Then I can't help myself; I scoot around to where she works on the backdrop to wipe away a tear newly resting against her cheek (leaving a bit of red paint in the process).

"It's insufficient, but I'm sorry. I didn't know you, yet I acted like a judge and jury, without any evidence, ready to condemn. I *still* can't believe some of the things I said, especially about a pregnancy. I don't want to be that kind of person, and it . . . it makes me feel sick."

She doesn't meet my eyes. "It's okay."

"No. It's not okay. I'm incredibly sorry, and I hope you'll forgive me."

Her head moves up and down, but she doesn't respond. Then she seems to pull herself together with a deep breath.

"You know what, Lola?"

I shake my head.

"You're not the only one who hurt me. *I've* been doing it all along!"

All of the sudden, she jumps up from the floor to start pacing, and as she talks, she punctuates each word with her hands.

"I have parents who care about me and teachers who encourage me—but what do I do? I go off and find a boyfriend who thinks I'm one step above a *roach*. And what do I do? Do I dump him? No. I believe him! I'm so angry with *myself!*" she cries out and gives another frustrated squeal, reminiscent of the one from our confrontation of weeks ago.

Then she deflates.

She almost falls into a nearby chair and sits there crumpled up, as still as a statue.

I shakily rise from my position on the floor and tiptoe to sit in a nearby chair.

"I've never felt like I belonged. I've always wanted to, but I never really felt like it. And I got tired of the feeling. I thought if I dated Matthew I would be able to fit in better, but instead it just backfired on me." In a much quieter voice, wistful eyes locked on the window, she says, "He would say the most *horrible* things to me."

I stay quiet. I'm not sure how to respond. I'm not sure if she's even really talking to me.

"It's okay. You don't have to say anything. I'm still trying to figure this all out myself," Jill continues.

"What can I do?" I ask.

"I'm not sure, but in a weird way, you've already helped. That day you confronted me . . . it was a huge wakeup call. And no, I'm not pregnant," she says and adds, "You're so strong, Lola. I wish I was strong like you."

She looks back at me with eyes much older than her age indicates.

"I'm sorry about George. He was a nice guy."

I nod and look away. I want to say that if she had been pregnant, I would hope to be the kind of person who would be a friend to her and value that baby.

I don't know how.

"Let's get back to work," she commands in a much firmer voice, and I think that sounds like a good idea.

"Pass me that charcoal pencil, please. You start on the green paint; then I'll take the black and try to add in some of the shading over the paint that's dried."

Mr. Atwood comes in a little while later to find us dry-eyed and working away together.

"Good work, girls," he comments in his typical calm manner.

I think it's the first time I've had a compliment from him. Ever. He must really like Jill.

CHAPTER 24

Operation Reconciliation is moving forward.

My next objective: corner Pumpkin.

I'm saving Jack for last. He's still giving me death glares.

So I continue to go to classes, work on homework, go to church on Sundays, and spend time with Grace on Wednesdays; but I know I have to talk to Pumpkin, and the sooner the better.

Then again, she's been a bit elusive.

I don't think it's on purpose like with Jill, so I try to relax. I try to be alert but not anxious.

It's difficult to wait, but I know God may have a reason for delaying this apology, so I work to be patient.

And in the process of waiting, I count my blessings. I endeavor not to think too much about how much I miss George.

I'm still often distracted, incidentally. Some things never change.

I notice posters for events shouting down from me on the walls of the school hallway . . . and a strange bird flying by on my way home with Charlotte and Earley . . . and some brightly colored Converse shoes Teresa has been wearing . . . and the patches all over the jacket of the guy who sits in front of me in study hall.

Who are the Ramones?

In this way, April arrives.

So one day as I'm running an errand for the study hall teacher to one of the coaches, I notice a poster I've never seen before by the entrance to the boys' gym.

It has a picture of George, and the poster board is looking a little worse for wear. I guess because, even though it's in a covered area, it's been outside the past couple of months.

The blue cardboard is spotted by rain, which has blown under the awning.

The splotches drip down like tears.

The purple ribbons are faded from the late afternoon sun.

But the picture itself is looking fine. It was laminated and hasn't suffered much damage.

He was so handsome, I think.

"He was handsome, wasn't he?" I hear a soft voice behind me.

Pumpkin steps up, puts her chin on my shoulder, and wraps her arms around my body.

"He was a really sweet guy, don't you think?" she asks.

I nod.

I don't know what to do or say, standing here with her comforting me.

We continue to look at the poster, but then Pumpkin does something else unexpected.

She lets me go, steps around me, and pulls the picture down.

"Here, Lola, I think you should have this. It's a really good shot. One of the yearbook staff photographers took it not long before Christmas break."

"Thanks," I scratch out as she rips the rest of the poster down and folds it in half to dump in the next available trash can.

And she's right. It's a great photo. It's a picture of George sitting at lunch, smiling archly across the table . . . at me. I'm not in it, but I almost always sat across from him, and I *know* that smile and the partially visible can of Tab, which hasn't been completely cropped out.

We were probably kidding each other about something.

This is *killing* me.

It's like finding your dearest treasure and realizing it's a knife to the heart—a beautiful, jewel-encrusted, needle-sharp knife.

"He really cared about you," Pumpkin whispers in my ear.

Without much effect, I wipe my tears, swallow, and nod once again.

I feel a tug on my hand, and I look up to find Pumpkin pulling me into the gym.

"You need to deliver something to the coach, I bet. Let's get that taken care of; then I'll walk you back to class. Okay?"

She leads me into the gym and deposits the faded poster board into a large trashcan sitting at the entrance. The gym is empty, even the office, but I drop the note in the overflowing inbox on the coach's desk. I hope he gets it.

"Come on," Pumpkin insists.

She gestures toward the door.

I follow.

"It's okay to still be sad, Lola. I'm still sad. He protected me—Jack told me he told you about what happened to me."

As we walk, I try to break my silence.

"I'm sor—"

But Pumpkin interrupts me with a shushing noise.

"You don't need to say you're sorry. I forgive you. I already forgave you, you know."

I shake my head. I didn't know.

"Well, I did. I was upset at first, but having to deal with a bunch of jealous, mean-spirited girls on the squad this year—well, at least you have a real reason to be unhappy. Anyway, you don't have to worry about me. I know you might not know me that well, but I feel like I know you. You're easy to know. You're so open and out there. It's refreshing. There's not much hidden with you. I like it."

And she graces me with her devastating smile.

"Thank you," I manage. Then I begin to cry in earnest.

Sometimes I know I don't deserve so much grace.

Thank you, God.

"God's good, isn't he?"

"Yes," I squeak.

How is she reading my mind?

She takes me by the arm and leads me to the Malignant Tumor, tugging me over to some benches built into one of the walls.

"Sit," she commands; then she sits down next to me, draws me in close, and pulls my head down to her shoulder, just as I did for Earley so many months ago.

"I think I have a Kleenex around here somewhere. I'm working as an office aide for this hour; they won't miss me for a while."

So she routes around her pockets and manages to find a clean one with hardly a wrinkle, which I quickly make as yucky as possible.

"Thanks, Pumpkin."

My voice is a little steadier now, so she lets me go.

"You're welcome," she responds in a subdued voice.

We sit there on these weird, carpeted benches, and it feels strange to be doing this at this time and in this place, but it doesn't stop us.

"Thank you for forgiving me."

"Of course I forgave you. I really care about you. Just like George cared about you."

I turn and crawl up to the next level, where I perch and sit cross-legged with my back to the mirrored wall; I clutch my picture and my tissue to my chest.

Pumpkin twists her body to face me.

"Pumpkin, why didn't you leave Sunset after what happened to you?"

"Well, that's a good question. My parents wanted to put me over at Bishop Dunne, but . . . well, gosh! It's my senior year, and I worked hard to get my position as captain, and I was pretty determined not to give it up."

"That makes sense. But how did you, George, and Jack keep the whole thing quiet?"

She sighs, looks down, and scratches her forehead.

"I'm not sure. None of us had ever seen the boys before, and no one has seen them since. As you know, well, it's an understatement to say I'm not a big talker. I asked George and Jack to keep it quiet and not to retaliate. And truthfully, we weren't one hundred percent sure who was responsible. My *parents* asked the principal to keep it quiet. There was talk of calling the police, but it never happened. I've wondered since if they weren't out-of-town friends or relatives of someone at the school, because the boys knew my name. I'm pretty sure now we'll never know where they came from. It's been so long, we've kinda relaxed our guard. The year is almost over, and with *that,* I think the motivation to come after me is almost over too. I think someone was trying to scare me out of being captain, but it got out of hand."

She's quiet a moment. "I'm not sure what would've taken place if Jack and George hadn't met up by chance and then found me. Those guys probably weren't serious in their threats anyway, or George and Jack wouldn't have been able to scare them off . . . I'm not sure."

This is the longest speech I've ever heard her give.

"Thanks for telling me."

It's her turn to nod. Then she smiles at me. "Come on. We better get you back to class." So we pull ourselves up and start the trek to study hall.

"Lola, I want you to come back to our lunch table, starting today."

My heart leaps for a moment, but then I say, "I'm not sure how Jack's going to feel about that."

"You know what? I don't care how he feels about it. Jack's a good guy, but he needs to stop pouting."

"I'll . . . give it a shot," I respond with a fair bit of hesitation.

She sets her beautiful mouth in a firm line and nods her attractive head emphatically to show her support as we arrive at the door to study hall.

Walking back in the room, I check my watch and realize I've been gone on my errand for about half an hour. I hope I don't get in trouble.

But as I wave good-bye to Pumpkin, the teacher doesn't even look up to acknowledge my return.

I really like study hall. The kids are different, but they don't stare, bother, or pick on me.

There's a lot to be said for that.

It's time for lunch.

I'm waffling on the decision to sit at my old table, but as soon as I enter the cafeteria, Pumpkin accosts me.

Believe it or not, she walks me through the line to get food and then carries my tray over to our table. She proceeds to drop it down between Lauri and Charlotte and pull out my chair. I have no choice other than to sit down and start eating.

"Hey, everyone," I give a weak greeting as I sit down.

I hear a chorus of expected responses, but one voice is conspicuous in its absence.

Once I'm brave enough to look in his direction (maybe I can diffuse the situation with a small, contrite smile), I see Jack not glaring at me but at Pumpkin.

The surprising thing is: she's glaring right back.

He pinches the bridge of his nose, sighs, and then pushes back his chair; he kicks it under the table and walks away, leaving his uneaten lunch.

"Don't worry, Lola. Be strong," Pumpkin commands.

I'm not sure what to do, but realizing her wisdom is greater than mine, I decide to let her lead the way, even as I feel a huge internal squirm at the thought.

"Okay," I croak and begin to pick at my food.

It helps when Charlotte gives me a hug; then Lauri starts joking about some loser in her science class who asked her on a date even though it's widely known he has a girlfriend.

"Can you believe his nerve?" she asks and then laughs her wonderful, deep laugh.

It's contagious, so we all laugh along with her.

It's a frivolous distraction, but it takes my mind off Jack . . . for now.

The next couple of weeks of Objective Four: Track Down Jack go like this:

I see him in the hall.

"Jack!"

He shakes his head and turns to leave. He won't even look at me!

I see Jack in the parking lot after school.

"Jack! Can I talk to you?"

"Leave me *alone*, Lola," he growls before fumbling into his big boat of a car and tearing out of the parking lot.

I see Jack at church.

"Jack. Please let me talk to you," I plead.

"*No*! I'm not forgiving you. You may've fooled everyone else, but I'll never forget what you've done." He turns on his heel and stalks away.

I stand there in what feels like alone. Then I leave to find my parents for a ride home.

"Grace, what do I do?" I ask her the next Wednesday night.

"Let me think about this for a minute, Lola," she says as she continues to brown meat for the tacos she's making for our dinner.

She clatters and splatters around the kitchen as she works. She cooks well enough, but I think the kitchen is the only place she's not graceful.

"Okay, I'm going to talk to you about some grownup stuff. Is that okay?" she says much later just as I've taken a big, crunchy bite of my first taco.

I manage to shake my head yes as sour cream drips down my chin.

"Okay," she sighs. "When Earley's dad left, my ex-husband, I'm sure you can imagine how devastated I felt."

This is serious stuff, so I nod my head yes and take another bite. I don't think I should answer.

"Earley was only three and a half, but he was still missing his daddy. Things hadn't been the best for a while, but up until then Howard had seemed stable. You know, committed. So for him to up and do something as cliché as run off with his secretary and then refuse to even talk to us or contact us except through his attorney . . . it was horrible."

I stop eating. I think I just lost my appetite.

"I'm sorry, Grace."

"Me too, but my whole point is that it was beyond my control. It would've helped if he had eventually asked for forgiveness. He never did. He did get back in touch with us after about a year and for Earley's sake, and for his own; I'm glad he did. At least Earley gets to spend a little time with him every summer in California, but . . . I'm sorry, I'm getting off track. My whole point is: It was beyond my control, and that's probably for the best. Otherwise, I sometimes still daydream about something to do with a public flogging."

She sighs before continuing. "I still get a little angry every now and then, but I've *chosen* to forgive him. That's all I can do. I can't make him say he's sorry. You've got a reverse situation, but you have to realize you can't make Jack forgive you. In fact, it sounds like it's getting to the point where you may have to exercise a little forgiveness toward him." She finishes; then she finally picks up her own taco and takes a bite.

"Do you have a good life, Grace? Are you happy?" I ask. I want to be reassured.

She nods a decisive yes as she crunches. I pick up my own and try to eat, but I'm thinking about little Earley crying for his dad.

It's heartbreaking.

But if Grace can forgive Howard, then it gives me hope Jack can forgive me.

And if Grace (who is good at *everything*) couldn't control her husband's actions; then it makes sense that I'm unable to control Jack's.

Grace swallows and takes a sip of her drink.

"Lola, I think you need to let it go for now. Let's pray God will give you discernment about when or *if* to approach him again. Okay?" She points at me with the remnant of her taco; then she smiles her reassuring smile.

"Okay, Grace. I'll try."

"Good. Eat, honey! I know this is a lot to think about, but your food is getting cold."

"Okay," I agree with a return smile that she has more than earned.

So we eat.

And I try to let it go.

For better or worse, it's actually not too difficult to put the situation with Jack aside once Grace advises me to do so.

It's almost as if I needed her permission.

After all, Grace always gives me good advice, and I'm easily sidetracked. And I have so many other things to think about, and to be grateful for.

I continue to sit with my friends at lunch; it makes me happy. George is still missing. Nothing is going to change that, but there's still contentment and laughter and togetherness.

My friends are helping me not to be so sad.

It's more than good.

And believe it or not, Jack rejoins the table after about a week.

He won't talk to me or look at me, and it's certain that his presence is grudging, but he's back.

So the days and weeks fly by; before we know it the school year is winding up.

"Oooo! Lola, I'm glad I found you. Sign my yearbook, please." Jill runs up to me with a hot-pink plumed pen in hand and her yearbook open.

"Sure! I'd be happy to. Here's mine. You sign it, okay?"

We trade books and scribble our brief thoughts.

I write: Dear Jill, Thank you for your forgiveness. Thank you for sharing your talent with me. Thank you for thinking I'm strong, even if I'm not. I hope we get to know each other better next year. Have a good summer! Lola.

She writes: Dear Lola, I just read over your shoulder, so I know you don't think you're strong, but you are. I think you're a nice person and look forward to getting to know you better in the future. Happy summer, Jill.

She adds a little picture of our old friend the garden gnome by her signature.

"Ha!" I laugh as I read over her entry. She's a funny, funny girl.

And before I know it, it's the end of the last day, and I'm walking toward Charlotte's car. I'm looking down at my yearbook and not where I'm walking, a bit risky, but . . .

"*Ow!*"

"Oh, no! I'm so sorry! Let me help you with your stuff." I'm frantic because, of all people, I've bumped into Jack. His belongings are all over the floor of the Malignant Tumor.

"No. I'll do it," he clips out.

"Please let me help, Jack. I'm *so* sorry for not watching where I was going," I implore.

"No. It's okay, Lola. I'm sure Charlotte is waiting for you. I'll get this." His response is quick to the point of rudeness.

I start sniffling.

"Okay. I'll leave you alone."

I can feel my mouth turn down and hear my voice get that wobbly sound, meaning I'm trying not to cry.

"But Jack, I just want to wish you luck . . . and tell you I'm sorry."

He won't look up, but he continues hunched over, gathering up his belongings.

"Whatever," he responds.

And with that reply I know I truly need to let it go, so I close my yearbook and start toward the door.

I may continue to cry over George every now and then, but I need to let the situation with Jack go.

Unless he decides to let me back into his life, these are the last tears I'll shed over him.

I care about Jack, but he's chosen not to forgive me. Grace is right; there's nothing further I can do about it.

So I straighten my shoulders and head out the door—out to blue skies, soon-to-be-intense heat, and my first post-George summer.

I'll survive.

I'll do better than survive.

Maybe Jill's right. Maybe I'm stronger than I think.

My light just may be shining.

EPILOGUE

We're barely into the summer (only two weeks).

Things are going okay.

Except Mom woke me up early about a week ago and told me I need to start looking for a job.

I haven't had much success yet, thank goodness. I'm not sure I'm ready for the kind of boring work I'm likely to land, but I'm trying to be diligent about the search.

So I drive around and go in various places to fill out applications.

I'm sure something will turn up before long. Unfortunately.

Until then, I'm catching up on my reading (I discovered *The Hobbit*), spending time with my friends, and sleeping in.

It's nice, actually.

Tonight, however, is a different matter. I'm excited and nervous all at the same time. The latest Star Trek movie came out about a week ago, and we've all been dying to see it. The gang went to see the first one together when it came out. So we're driving over to the Wynnewood this evening for just that purpose.

The only problem is Jack.

He's still ignoring me. I don't like it, but I guess it's better than the glares.

Consequently, I try to ignore him back—it just seems practical. But as it's been mentioned before, he's a huge Star Trek fan.

He saw it on opening night but wouldn't miss the opportunity to see the movie a second time with his friends (and one nonfriend).

Even David, Jack's best friend who's home from college, will be meeting us there.

I hope David's not mad at me too.

Actually, it crossed my mind not to go, but this might be my only chance to see the movie. After all, Charlotte will give me a ride to see it while my parents most certainly will not. At least, I don't think so.

I even voiced my concerns about Jack to Charlotte, Lauri, and Teresa earlier today while spending time at the mall and filling out applications.

"I really want to go with you to the movie tonight, but I'm not sure that Jack will be able to handle it. I'm not sure *I* can handle Jack not handling it."

"You have to go!" Charlotte pleads before adding, "It's a tradition, or, I guess, it will be after this time. There's only been one other Star Trek movie."

"I think you should go," Teresa contributes her agreement with a smile.

"Seriously? You're thinking about staying home because Jack's still angry with you? You just need to buck up and go," Lauri, the voice of practicality, interjects.

"Oh! Look at that dress! Isn't it pretty?" I respond.

"Don't try to change the subject."

"Okay, okay! I'll go. Is everyone satisfied now?"

The words absolutely, perfectly, and *yippee!* chime out in unison.

So that's that, I decide.

"Majority rules, I guess. I'll just try to stay out of his way," I say to no one in particular.

They nod, and we continue to window shop. None of us ever have much money to buy clothes, anyway.

Well, I can't help but be excited.

I don't want to make Jack uncomfortable, but it's fun to go to the movies with friends.

"David! How're you doing? How is college?" I ask our summertime friend.

We're standing out in the front of the theater waiting for the rest of the group to arrive.

Dad allowed me to borrow his car tonight; instead of Charlotte having to backtrack, I've brought Earley, Teresa, and Lauri with me.

"It's going weeeell . . ." he trails off as he begins to squint at something behind me.

I flip around to see Jack and Pumpkin walk up.

They're holding hands.

This makes me want to giggle (she's so much taller than he), so I quickly flip back around before Jack can see me.

"Hey, Jack, Pumpkin. This is a new development," David remarks as they walk up.

I compose myself and slowly turn back around. Pumpkin's beaming. Jack is looking a little self-conscious. Then he spots me, and his eyes narrow.

I step back behind Earley in order to hide; I guess no one told Jack I would be here.

"I'm *leaving!*" Jack sounds disgusted.

"What? We can't leave! It's our first date! It's my first date *ever*, and you're going to *ruin* it!" Pumpkin wails.

I cower closer in behind Teresa and Earley.

"Lola, what are you doing back there?" Earley whispers; then I feel him begin to shake with laughter.

"Hiding," I hiss.

The bickering from the new couple continues in the background.

"Hiding?" Teresa exclaims in surprise.

I suddenly feel a hand on my arm pulling me out into the open.

It's Pumpkin; she looks livid.

Not so amazing, she still looks good.

"Okay, you two. Listen up and listen well. We're not playing around like this anymore. Lola, you're *not* hiding. And Jack, you're *not* leaving. Get over yourselves. Gee whiz," she dictates, suddenly the boss of the universe. I guess this is how she got all the recalcitrant cheerleaders to do her bidding.

"Yeah, Jack, get over yourself," David snickers and continues, "what is going on with these two, anyway?"

"It's a long story. But the movie is about to start. We better get tickets and get in our seats. We don't want to miss the previews," Teresa wisely advises.

So we line up at the ticket window, and before you know it, the movie has started.

And the really weird part: I've somehow ended up seated next to Jack.

I promise it was an accident. I'm not sure how it happened. I tried to walk in with Lauri, Charlotte, and David so I wouldn't be getting in between the couples, but I became distracted by another movie's poster and ended up at the back of the group, right behind Jack.

Everyone else was already packed in like sardines.

I started to sit on another row. But Pumpkin caught me trying to make my escape and with a simple hand gesture pretty much assured my compliance.

I've rarely seen this side of her before.

It's scary.

Jack is practically leaning all over her in his desire to get away from me in the cramped space.

"Jack, scoot over!" she softly but sternly commands.

I can't help it. I have to laugh—and I put away my sheepishness for good. It's not helped.

"Yeah, Jack. I don't bite. Well, not very *hard*." Good grief! This is getting ridiculous even by my standards.

My response causes the whole row to crack up, so I join right in. Then other, more serious members of the audience hush us.

The movie starts.

It's good, I think. I'm wondering if that's Ricardo Montalban's real chest, but still, it's really good.

I can't believe this—Spock is sacrificing himself to save the rest of the crew!

Spock can't die.

Save him, Dr. McCoy!

This is the future; there has to be something they can do.

This is making me sad.

Then Scotty is playing "Amazing Grace" on the bagpipes, and that's all it takes for me to start bawling.

For once, I have no Kleenex in my purse. I guess I'll use my sleeve.

Then out of the blue, there's a tissue floating in front of my face.

Thank goodness! I say to myself as I grab it.

Oh! It's Jack.

"Thanks, Pumpkin," I lean up to whisper to her, assuming he just passed it over. "It's not from Pumpkin. It's from me," Jack murmurs back.

I glance over in bewilderment and sit back.

Then I notice the light from the screen reflecting off his face. There's one tiny teardrop making its slow way down his right cheek.

I swallow.

"Thanks, Jack."

He nods his head once.

And I remember George was his best friend too.

After the movie, David kids me about crying over Spock's death, but the rest of my friends remain quiet.

They know how much I still cry.

I guess David's been so removed at college, he's temporarily forgotten our loss.

He's temporarily forgotten our George.

That's understandable, I guess.

"Let's get ice cream and take it to the park," Earley suggests.

He must sense that we're not ready to go home yet.

"That's a great idea," Pumpkin seconds, and with the way she's been bossing us around tonight, everyone will now fall in line.

So we get our ice cream at Baskin-Robbins and drive to Kiest Park to sit on the swings as we eat.

We drift over to the merry-go-round, my favorite.

The boys push us; we twirl so fast it feels as if we're going to fly off. We're barely hanging on.

Then at one point, we slow. Pumpkin and Jack walk over to sit on a bench. I lay down in the middle of the merry-go-round as it revolves.

It's a clear night; I can see the moon and stars as I turn.

They're breathtaking.

We finally stop spinning; David drifts away.

Pumpkin and Jack continue to sit on their park bench. David stands close by them, and they discuss the movie and other things. I think I hear one of the boys ask about her real name. Her funny little snort sounds out in the dark, quiet air.

Teresa and Lauri amble back over to the swings. They swing so high their toes will soon touch the bright, untouchable moon.

Earley, Charlotte, and I continue on the merry-go-round. Soon they lay down on either side of me.

"Why did George have to die?" I ask the sky.

"I'm not sure, Lola," Earley replies. I feel Charlotte shrug on my other side.

"Do you think it hurt?" I dare to ask on a swallow.

My eyes are barely dry.

"I don't think so," Charlotte answers. Her voice is gentle. "My mom told me it was quick. I don't know if you remember, but it was raining that night. Some people ran out into the street in front of his car, and he swerved to avoid them. It was an accident. They weren't looking; they didn't see him coming. It was a thirteen-year-old, a preschooler, and their mother. At least, that's what my parents said."

"That's what I heard too," Earley says.

"I'm glad they're okay. You know, the family," I manage after a long pause.

Then I grab their hands, and we continue to stargaze.

"God loves us. I know we don't have the answer to this, but God loves us. I'm sure of it." Charlotte squeezes my hand.

"God loves us," I repeat; my voice cracks. But my heart is sure.

"Yes, God loves us," Earley whispers in what sounds like a prayer.

So we continue to look at the mystery of the sky and contemplate the mystery and uncertainty of life.

So much is beyond our comprehension and control.

So much is fragile.

But we have each other.

"Let's go home." Earley pulls me up, and I pull Charlotte up in turn.

"Let's go home!" he loudly repeats to the group.

So we do.

ACKNOWLEDGMENTS

Encouragement is like dark chocolate—I never seem to get enough. So I would like to thank those who've fed it to my insatiable, prose-loving monster.

Thanks to Pastor Brian Carroll, who was the first non-family member to compliment my writing and allow me to contribute a piece of my heart to our church.

Thank you to Staci Levine, my Bisonette little sis, a brush with greatness, and a shoo-in to win gold if hugging was an Olympic event, for taking the time to meet with me and encourage my writing. It was too long ago.

Thank you to those who read early drafts, including Robin Walls, Michelle Delaune, and Marianne Little. Many thanks to those who read later versions, including my third child, Tyler Whigham; fantastic neighbor, Kristi Gray; and partner-in-crime, the multitalented Lori Horb, who later brought Lola to life and sent her to me for my birthday.

Thank you to Kristi Coleman for a friendship spanning many decades, her outstanding memory, her love of stories, and being the first person to give me honest, helpful critique on my original manuscript. Thanks are also due her daughter, Corrie, for bringing that wonderful Warren Leslie quote to light.

Une mille merci to mon amie, Katie Pothier, for continuing to call me Lola even though it's been years since her daughter mispronounced my name.

Thank you to my incredi-husband Craig Angaroni, who read every draft I asked of him without complaint. Thank you for being my support when I've cried over this book and for sharing my fun when I've laughed over it. I would expect nothing less, of course, because that's what good husbands do.

It warms me when I think of the pride my children will take in this publication. Emma and Andrew, thank you for being the best teenagers for whom a parent could ever hope. How do you manage that?

I wish to thank our parents, David and Nellie Porterfield and Al and Marie Angaroni, for raising us in faithful households and for encouraging even the tiniest blip of potential detected in us over the years.

Thanks to my sister, Lisa Estep, who, in my eyes, hung the moon. I'll keep writing if you keep snapping pictures, Batgirl.

I would like to thank Bill Carmichael of Deep River Books for giving me the opportunity to publish my book, and Andy Carmichael for coordinating the beautiful cover and understanding why I wanted to name the book *Lowly*. I would also like to thank Kit Tosello for answering multitudes of questions, liking unusual Italian last names, and understanding the need to take time out to play Pokémon Go with my teens.

I wish to express huge thanks to my editor, Rachel Starr Thomson, for thinking my book was beautiful. You won me over at the word *love*. In fact, I'll trade you my slice of Canadian bacon (no, it's ham!) pizza for a slice of your Canadian pizza. You just tell me where and when.

God's the author of everything good, including creativity. I love this. Thank you, Father, for giving me the blessing of purpose, a quiet joy, and a way to help, and in a manner that I never imagined before I sat down in front of my computer and started typing.

AUTHOR'S PAGE

Laura Angaroni was raised in the Oak Cliff section of Dallas and is proud to be from what some would consider the wrong side of the tracks. She attended Baylor University, where she acquired her economics degree and met her cute, New Jersey-born husband, Craig. Their first kiss was at the bear pit, and it wasn't long before she decided it wouldn't be so bad to have a last name that might be confused with a type of pasta.

Their many adventures include the birth of their firstborn, a daughter, and later, a seven-year-long vacation in Montreal, Quebec, Canada, where their son was born.

They've since touched down in the Houston orbit. Laura writes, coaches her teens, reads too much, and distracts the librarian at her son's school with chitchat instead of shelving books. She just completed a four-year commitment with her church's high school ministry and plans to chase preschoolers around the church nursery for a bit before returning to work with young adults.

Find out more about Laura at https://laurapangaroni.com.

CPSIA information can be obtained
at www.ICGtesting.com
Printed in the USA
FSOW01n1953290317
32322FS